INSTANT
Spanish
Vocabulary Builder
with Online Audio

T0275275

INSTANT
Spanish
Vocabulary Builder
with Online Audio

TOM MEANS, PH.D.

HIPPOCRENE BOOKS, INC.
NEW YORK

Audio files available at www.hippocrenebooks.com

Online audio edition, 2018.
Text copyright © 2003 Tom Means
Audio copyright © 2003 Hippocrene Books, Inc.

Book design by Acme Klong Design.

For information, address:
HIPPOCRENE BOOKS, INC.
171 Madison Avenue
New York, NY 10016
www.hippocrenebooks.com

Previous edition ISBN: 978-0-7818-0981-8

Cataloging-in-publication data available from the Library of Congress.

ISBN 978-0-7818-1374-7

CONTENTS

	English suffix	Spanish suffix	Page
Chapter 1	–al*	–al	1
Chapter 2	–ance	–ancia	15
Chapter 3	–ant	–ante	19
Chapter 4	–ar	–ar	25
Chapter 5	–ary	–ario	29
Chapter 6	–ble	–ble	35
Chapter 7	–ct	–cto	47
Chapter 8	–ence	–encia	53
Chapter 9	–ent**	–ente	61
Chapter 10	–gy	–gía	69
Chapter 11	–ic	–ico	75
Chapter 12	–ical	–ico	89
Chapter 13	–id	–ido	97
Chapter 14	–ism	–ismo	101

Audio files available for download at:
http://www.hippocrenebooks.com/instant-spanish-vocabulary-builder.html

*excluding words ending in "–ical," which is a separate Chapter
**excluding words ending in "–ment," which is a separate Chapter

ACKNOWLEDGMENTS

I would like to give special thanks to Juan Pablo Lombana, whose research and bilingual expertise helped make this book possible.

Many thanks to Angelica Bender for her technical assistance with the entire series. Thanks to Ernest Valdés, Enid Bender, Diana Murgio, Dr. Karen Sanchez, John Carleo, and all of my students at Kenneth Cole Productions. Thanks to my editor, Anne Kemper, for her steady and enthusiastic guidance, and also to my former editor, Caroline Gates.

Finally, thanks to all the foreign language teachers who have clearly demonstrated many of these patterns in the past, especially Margarita Madrigal and Michel Thomas.

HOW WE LEARN LANGUAGES

Learning languages is at once a simple yet complex process. It's simple because in essence, we really only need to hear and see a language in order to learn it. If we hear and see a language often enough in contexts that are meaningful to us, we will eventually begin speaking and writing it.

It's complex because the human brain needs to see and hear the language for hundreds and hundreds of hours before it can start to make sense of its patterns and rules. If you can watch/read/listen to the new language enough times, then you can learn it. The ways in which you're exposed to a new language, however, must be meaningful to you in order to be memorable and impact your learning.

So it's complex but not impossible—just find speakers, books, videos, games, music, etc. in the new language and watch/play/read/listen to these resources every day. If the sources you use are memorable and meaningful to you and you have prolonged exposure to them, then after hundreds of hours spent with the new language, your brain will tell your mouth what to do, and abracadabra (!) you will be speaking this new language for the rest of your life.

There are only four ways to become exposed to a new language, so you don't have to worry about how to get started or how to continue toward your goal. The four modalities of language learning are READING, SPEAKING, LISTENING, and WRITING. This book and audio program provide some practice with all four modalities.

In order to learn a language, the first steps and most impactful modalities are LISTENING and READING. These allow learners to collect information (the other two modalities, speaking and writing, are aimed at producing the language once you get some "gas" in the tank). I strongly recommend watching television or movies in the new language. Here's the most important part: You will not understand everything you hear (sometimes it will feel like you don't understand anything!) but your brain will be making sense of all this valuable information so that it can eventually comprehend it and produce it. Try to find a TV program and dozens of movies that interest you in the new language. Watch them with a regular routine, even if it's only thirty minutes per day. And most importantly, keep watching and listening when you don't understand what they're saying! Your brain will make sense of it all but it needs the "nutrition" of hundreds of hours of input to make sense of it. Feed your brain the new language every day.

This book/online audio program provides obvious examples for listening and reading—read the words out loud in each chapter and listen to the examples and stories in each chapter. The reason I emphasize listening and reading first is because that's how we all learned our first language. Babies don't speak or write in their language until they've heard it and seen it for several years. This is very similar to what your brain needs for your new language. There are some differences between how a baby learns a first language and how children and adults learn second/third languages, but the fundamental requirement of hearing and seeing the language in abundance is the same for both.

The other two modalities are also important: you need to practice SPEAKING and WRITING in the new language in order to develop advanced levels of communication. This book/online audio program provides opportunities to practice writing and speaking—especially in the four exercises that end each of the chapters. You will be challenged to match words and to write simple sentences about the stories. For speaking, you should imitate the native speaker as he/she pronounces the words and expressions in every chapter (they are all set in **bold**), and you can also read the stories out loud to practice your pronunciation.

Lastly, I want to emphasize the importance of patience. Your brain can learn any language and it will do it very gradually. You only need to do four things, as summarized here:

- **Listen to/watch the language in material that interests you.** Keep watching even when you don't understand everything. After hundreds of hours of this, your brain will reward your efforts with understanding.

- **Read the language in material that interests you.** This can be anything that is written in the language: song lyrics, cartoons, illustrated books, magazines, websites, word games, etc. Keep reading because this will also help your ears eventually understand the listening task better.

- **Speak the language and make sure that what you are saying is important to you.** Practice speaking with a real person about your life, your family, your goals, your challenges. As you speak to someone, they will naturally respond and then you will also be working on your listening. Even if you can't find a conversation partner right now, imitate how people speak—when you are home, you can imitate people from videos and online speech.

- **Write the language and make sure you are writing about things that are authentic.** For example, try to write a description of your daily routine, your family, your residence, etc. If possible, find someone to provide you with some instruction. It does not have to be formal instruction but you will need some guidance.

For more information on these tips, please watch some videos on my YouTube channel, "Professor JT Means." If you have discipline, patience and interest in the new language (and you follow these steps) progress is inevitable.

INTRODUCTION

nstant Spanish Vocabulary Builder can add thousands of words to your Spanish vocabulary. It is designed to be a supplement for students of Spanish at all levels. This book will help a student to learn to communicate effectively by dramatically increasing his/her Spanish vocabulary.

There are thousands of English words that are connected to their Spanish counterparts by word-ending patterns. This guide will illustrate those patterns and demonstrate how easily they work. The simple reason is that most of Spanish and much of English is derived from Latin. This means that the two languages share a large number of root words, which makes vocabulary building much easier.

Vocabulary building is one of the keys for successful language learning. This book presents vocabulary patterns between English and Spanish in such a systematic fashion that expanding your vocabulary will be easy and enjoyable. I believe it is the only one of its kind.

Instant Spanish Vocabulary Builder is very easy to use. The 24 patterns presented in this book are based on word-endings (suffixes) and the chapters are listed alphabetically. For example, the first chapter presents English words that end in "–al" (capital, normal, etc.) Many of these words end in "–al" in Spanish also (capital, normal, etc.)

The second chapter presents English words that end in "–ance" (distance, importance, etc.) Many of these words correspond to "–ancia" in Spanish (distancia, importancia, etc.) In most cases, you only need to slightly change the ending of the English word to arrive at the correct Spanish word. These words are commonly referred to as cognates: words related by common derivation or descent.

AUDIO ACCOMPANIMENT: This book comes with online audio accompaniment which is available for free download. Every chapter contains many recorded words that typify how words under that pattern are pronounced—all words **in bold** are on the recording. After each Spanish word there will be a pause—it is important for the reader to imitate the native speaker during that pause.

Every chapter also contains common phrases and expressions that are recorded on the audio accompaniment. After every recorded expression there will be a pause for the reader to imitate the native speaker. All expressions **in bold** are on the recording.

In the exercise section of each chapter there are stories for the student to read and listen to with questions that follow. These stories are **in bold** and are also on the recording. They are read by a native speaker at standard speed. Readers are not expected to understand every word of each story, but it is important for language learners to hear new vocabulary words used in an authentic context by a native speaker.

EXERCISES: At the end of every chapter, there are exercises for the reader to do. The first exercise is a matching exercise that reinforces the new words learned in the chapter. The second exercise is a story followed by questions. Every chapter contains a short story about Juan and Angélica, two young Spaniards traveling through Spain.

ANSWER KEY: Answers for the exercises are available in the Answer Key section.

INSTANT Spanish Vocabulary Builder

"FALSE FRIENDS":
Sometimes the English word and the Spanish word will look alike and sound alike, but have different meanings. These are often referred to as "false friends" or "false cognates." When this is the case, a more appropriate definition will be provided alongside the translation. One such example can be seen with the English word "parent."

ENGLISH . . . . SPANISH

parent . . . . pariente (meaning "a relative")

In some rare cases, the English and Spanish word possess such different meanings that the pair was not included in this book. For example, the meaning of the English word "journal" has no relation to the meaning of the Spanish word jornal (day's pay). In other rare cases, overly technical words were not included in this book.

DEVIATIONS IN SPELLING:
Precise spelling of the Spanish words may differ from the English words in more ways than just the endings. If you are interested in spelling the word correctly, please pay close attention to the Spanish column. For example,

ENGLISH . . . . SPANISH

dictionary . . . . diccionario

PRONUNCIATION GUIDE: All bolded words in this brief

pronunciation guide are recorded on the accompanying audio, **track 25.**

There are 27 letters in the Spanish alphabet (one more than in the English alphabet). The additional letter is "ñ." Listed below is a brief guide to Spanish pronunciation. English equivalent sounds have been provided whenever possible.

Spanish vowel	Example	Approximate English sound
A	**España**	ah
E	**excelente**	eh
I	**día**	ee
O	**loco**	oh
U	**mucho**	oooh

There are a few pairings that produce distinct sounds that we will go over next:

"ce" and "ci" always produce a soft sound like the English letter "s": **cena** (dinner); **cita** (appointment)

The pairing "ge" produces a soft sound similar to the word "head": **gente** (people)
The pairing "gi" produces a sound similar to the word "he": **giro** (turn)

"ca" produces a hard sound similar to the word "car": **casa** (house)
"co" sounds approximately like the beginning of "colon": **código** (code)
"cu" produces a hard sound similar to the word "cool": **cubo** (bucket)

"ga" sounds approximately like the beginning of "garbage": **ganar** (to win/to earn)

"go" produces a hard sound similar to the word "going": **gota** (drop)

"gu" produces a hard sound similar to the word "guru": **gula** (gluttony)

"gui" sounds approximately like the word "gear": **guitarra** (guitar)

"gue" produces a hard sound similar to the word "ghetto": **guerrero** (warrior)

The "cc" pairing usually produces a sound similar to "x" in the word "ax": **acción** (action)

The "je" pairing sounds similar to the word "hedge": **jefe** (boss)

The "ll" sounds like the "ll" in "tortilla": **pasillo** (hallway)

The "ñ" sounds like the "ny" in "canyon": **años** (years)

Lastly, the letter "h" is silent in Spanish: **hasta** (until)

IMPORTANT NOTE ON GENDER: Unless otherwise noted in the chapter introduction, all Spanish nouns and adjectives listed in this book are in the singular, masculine form. All nouns are listed without the article that typically accompanies them.

WORKS CONSULTED

Larousse Diccionario Español-Ingles, Ingles-Español. Primera Edicion.
México D.F., México: Larousse, 1999.

Merriam-Webster's Collegiate Dictionary, Tenth Edition. Springfield, MA:
Merriam-Webster, 2000.

Vox, Diccionario General de la Lengua Española (CD-ROM). Barcelona,
Spain: Bibliograf, 1997.

Devney, Dorothy M. Guide to Spanish Suffixes. Chicago: Passport Books,
1992.

Knorre, Marty; Dorwick, Thalia; Perez-Girones, Ana Maria; Glass, William
R.; Villareal, Hildebrando. Puntos de Partida, Fifth Edition. Boston:
McGraw-Hill, 1997.

Madrigal, Margarita. Margarita's Magical Key to Spanish. New York:
Doubleday, 1989.

Prado, Marcial. NTC's Dictionary of Spanish False Cognates. Chicago,
NTC Publishing Group, 1993.

Thomas, Michel. Spanish with Michel Thomas. Chicago: NTC Publishing
Group, 2000.

A NOTE FROM THE AUTHOR

When I first started studying Spanish, I translated an old trick I had learned from Italian: most English words that end in "–tion" stay the same in Spanish but their ending changes to "–ción." I was soon confidently speaking of the new "situación" that I had seen at the "estación," or about the "condición" of this or that. I was convinced that I had found the "solución" to speaking Spanish!

I know that this vocabulary bridge aided my Spanish skills greatly and fed my enthusiasm for learning and using a beautiful language.

In this book I have collected the 24 most common and applicable vocabulary bridges that exist between English and Spanish. I have done this in the hope that readers find the same immediate application that I did early in my language studies. I hope you find them useful.

A NOTE TO THE USER

The focus of this book is on vocabulary development. However, as with all effective language materials, the vocabulary has been set in an authentic cultural context with realistic characters and stories to encourage immediate applicability in real-life situations.

The exercises are suitable for individual and group work. Teachers will find that the 24 chapters easily can be incorporated into a one-year curriculum.

Chapter 1

Many English words ending in "–al" have the same ending in Spanish (excluding words ending in "–ical," which is a separate pattern).

Spanish words ending in "–al" are usually adjectives or nouns. For example,

artificial (adj.) = *artificial*
animal (n.) = *un animal*

ENGLISH . . . . SPANISH

All words and phrases in **bold** *are on* **Track 1** *of the accompanying audio.*

abdominal . . . . abdominal
abnormal . . . . anormal
accidental . . . . accidental
actual . . . . actual *(meaning "current, present")*
additional . . . . adicional
adverbial . . . . adverbial
amoral . . . . amoral
ancestral . . . . ancestral
animal . . . . **animal**
　　"It's an animal!" . . . . **"¡Es un animal!"**
annual . . . . anual
antiliberal . . . . antiliberal
antisocial . . . . antisocial
arsenal . . . . arsenal
artificial . . . . artificial
asexual . . . . asexual
asocial . . . . asocial
audiovisual . . . . audiovisual
autumnal . . . . otoñal

banal	banal
baptismal	bautismal
beneficial	beneficial *(more commonly "beneficioso")*
bestial	bestial
biannual	bianual
biennial	bienal
bifocal	bifocal
bilateral	bilateral
bisexual	bisexual
bronchial	bronquial
brutal	**brutal**

"It's a brutal reaction.". . . . . . **"Es una reacción brutal".**

canal	canal *(also used for "TV channel")*
cannibal	caníbal
capital	**capital** *(for geography, use "la capital"; for finance, use "el capital")*
cardinal	cardinal
carnal	carnal
carnival	carnaval *(also used for period of Mardi Gras)*
casual	casual *(also used for "by chance")*
cathedral	catedral
causal	causal
celestial	celestial
central	**central**
cereal	cereal
cerebral	cerebral
ceremonial	ceremonial
choral	coral
circumstantial	circunstancial
coincidental	coincidencial
collateral	colateral
colloquial	coloquial
colonial	colonial

INSTANT Spanish Vocabulary Builder

colossal . . . . colosal
commercial. . . . . comercial
communal. . . . . comunal
conceptual . . . . conceptual
conditional . . . . condicional
confessional . . . . confesional *(only an adjective)*
confidential. . . . . confidencial
confrontational . . . . confrontacional
constitutional. . . . . constitucional
contextual. . . . . contextual
continental . . . . **continental**
contractual . . . . contractual
controversial . . . . controversial
conventional . . . . convencional
conversational. . . . . conversacional
coral . . . . coral
cordial . . . . cordial
corporal . . . . corporal
corral. . . . . corral
correctional . . . . correccional
cranial . . . . craneal
credential . . . . credencial
criminal . . . . criminal
crucial . . . . **crucial**
   "Tomorrow is a crucial day." . . . . **"Mañana es un día crucial"**.
crystal . . . . cristal
cultural. . . . . cultural

decimal . . . . decimal
dental . . . . dental
departmental. . . . . departamental
devotional . . . . devocional
diagonal. . . . . **diagonal**
dictatorial. . . . . dictatorial
differential . . . . diferencial
digital . . . . digital

dimensional . . . . dimensional
disloyal . . . . desleal
divisional . . . . divisional
doctoral . . . . doctoral
dorsal . . . . dorsal
dual . . . . dual
ducal . . . . ducal
dysfunctional . . . . disfuncional

editorial . . . . editorial
electoral . . . . electoral
elemental . . . . elemental *(meaning "elementary")*
emotional . . . . emocional
episcopal . . . . episcopal
equal . . . . **igual**
equatorial . . . . ecuatorial
essential . . . . esencial
eternal . . . . eternal *(more commonly "eterno")*
eventual . . . . eventual *(meaning "possible")*
exceptional . . . . excepcional
existential . . . . existencial
experimental . . . . experimental
exponential . . . . exponencial
extramarital . . . . extramatrimonial

facial . . . . facial
factual . . . . factual
fatal . . . . fatal *(also used for "terrible," "lousy")*
federal . . . . federal
festival . . . . festival
fetal . . . . fetal
feudal . . . . feudal
filial . . . . filial
final . . . . **final**
fiscal . . . . fiscal
floral . . . . floral

focal . . . . focal
formal . . . . formal
fraternal . . . . fraternal
frontal . . . . frontal
frugal. . . . . frugal
functional . . . . funcional
fundamental . . . . **fundamental**
funeral . . . . funeral

gastrointestinal . . . . gastrointestinal
general . . . . **general**
generational . . . . generacional
genial . . . . genial *(meaning "talented," "brilliant")*
germinal. . . . . germinal
glacial . . . . glacial
global . . . . global
gradual . . . . gradual
grammatical . . . . gramatical
gravitational . . . . gravitacional
guttural. . . . . gutural

habitual . . . . habitual
heterosexual . . . . heterosexual
homosexual . . . . homosexual
horizontal. . . . . horizontal
hormonal . . . . hormonal
hospital . . . . **hospital**

ideal . . . . **ideal**
illegal. . . . . **ilegal**
     "Stealing is illegal.". . . . . **"Robar es ilegal".**
immaterial . . . . inmaterial
immoral . . . . inmoral
immortal. . . . . inmortal
impartial. . . . . imparcial
imperial . . . . imperial

impersonal . . . . impersonal
inaugural . . . . inaugural
incidental . . . . incidental
individual . . . . individual *(adjective only;*
                                        noun is "individuo")
industrial . . . . industrial
infernal . . . . infernal
informal . . . . informal
initial . . . . **inicial**
institutional . . . . institucional
instrumental . . . . instrumental
insubstantial . . . . insustancial
integral . . . . integral
intellectual . . . . intelectual
intentional. . . . . intencional
intercontinental . . . . intercontinental
international . . . . **internacional**
     "It's an international   **"Es una compañía**
     company." . . . . **internacional".**
interpersonal. . . . . interpersonal
interracial. . . . . interracial
intestinal. . . . . intestinal
irrational . . . . irracional

jovial . . . . jovial
judicial. . . . . judicial

labial . . . . labial
lateral . . . . lateral
latitudinal . . . . latitudinal
legal . . . . **legal**
lethal . . . . letal
liberal . . . . liberal
literal . . . . literal

local . . . . local *(also used as "commercial premises")*

longitudinal. . . . . longitudinal

loyal . . . . leal

manual. . . . . manual

marginal. . . . . marginal

marital . . . . marital

martial . . . . marcial

material . . . . material

maternal. . . . . maternal

matriarchal. . . . . matriarcal

matrimonial . . . . matrimonial

medicinal . . . . medicinal

medieval . . . . medieval

menstrual . . . . menstrual

mental . . . . **mental**

    "It's a mental problem." . . . . . **"Es un problema mental".**

meridional . . . . meridional *(meaning "Southern")*

metal . . . . metal

mineral. . . . . mineral

modal . . . . modal

monumental . . . . monumental

moral. . . . . moral

mortal . . . . mortal

multicultural . . . . multicultural

multifunctional. . . . . multifuncional

multinational. . . . . multinacional

municipal . . . . municipal

mural. . . . . mural

musical. . . . . musical

mutual . . . . mutual *(more commonly "mutuo")*

nasal . . . . nasal

natal . . . . natal

national . . . . **nacional**
natural . . . . natural
naval . . . . naval
Neanderthal . . . . neandertal
neutral . . . . neutral
nominal . . . . nominal
normal . . . . normal
numeral . . . . numeral
nuptial . . . . nupcial
nutritional . . . . nutricional

occasional . . . . ocasional *(also used for "accidental")*
occidental . . . . occidental *(meaning "Western")*
occupational . . . . ocupacional
octagonal . . . . octagonal
official . . . . oficial
operational . . . . operacional
optional . . . . opcional
oral . . . . oral
ordinal . . . . ordinal
organizational . . . . organizacional
oriental . . . . oriental *(meaning "Eastern")*
original . . . . **original**
ornamental . . . . ornamental
oval . . . . oval

papal . . . . papal
paranormal . . . . paranormal
parochial . . . . parroquial
partial . . . . parcial
pastoral . . . . pastoral
patrimonial . . . . patrimonial
pectoral . . . . pectoral
pedal . . . . pedal
pedestal . . . . pedestal
penal . . . . penal

personal . . . . personal
phenomenal . . . . fenomenal
plural . . . . plural
portal . . . . portal
positional . . . . posicional
postal . . . . postal
postnatal . . . . postnatal
potential . . . . potencial
preferential . . . . preferencial
prenatal . . . . prenatal
prenuptial . . . . prenupcial
prepositional . . . . preposicional
presidential . . . . presidencial
primordial . . . . primordial
principal . . . . **principal**
procedural . . . . procedimental
processional . . . . procesional
professional . . . . profesional
promotional . . . . promocional
proportional . . . . proporcional
proverbial . . . . proverbial
providential . . . . providencial
provincial . . . . provincial
provisional . . . . provisional
punctual . . . . puntual

racial . . . . racial
radial . . . . radial
radical . . . . radical
rational . . . . racional
real . . . . real
recital . . . . recital
regional . . . . **regional**
relational . . . . relacional
residential . . . . residencial
residual . . . . residual

reverential . . . . reverencial
ritual . . . . ritual
rival . . . . rival
royal . . . . real
rural . . . . rural

sacramental . . . . sacramental
sacrificial . . . . sacrificial
sculptural . . . . escultural
semifinal . . . . semifinal
seminal . . . . seminal
senatorial . . . . senatorial
sensational . . . . sensacional
sensual . . . . sensual
sentimental . . . . sentimental
sepulchral . . . . sepulcral
sequential . . . . secuencial
sexual . . . . sexual
signal . . . . señal
social . . . . **social**
sociocultural . . . . sociocultural
spatial . . . . espacial
special . . . . **especial**
spinal . . . . espinal
spiral . . . . espiral
spiritual . . . . espiritual
structural . . . . estructural
subliminal . . . . subliminal
substantial . . . . sustancial
subtotal . . . . subtotal
subtropical . . . . subtropical
superficial . . . . superficial
supernatural . . . . supernatural
surreal . . . . surreal

tangential . . . . tangencial

temperamental . . . . temperamental
temporal. . . . . temporal *(also used for
"temporary"
and "storm")*
terminal . . . . terminal
territorial . . . . territorial
testimonial . . . . testimonial
textual . . . . textual
thermal. . . . . termal *(meaning "related to springs")*
tonal . . . . tonal
torrential. . . . . torrencial
total. . . . . **total**
traditional. . . . . tradicional
transcendental. . . . . trascendental
transcontinental. . . . . transcontinental
transitional . . . . transicional
transsexual . . . . transexual
tribal . . . . tribal
tribunal . . . . tribunal *(meaning "courthouse")*
trivial . . . . trivial
tropical. . . . . **tropical**

unconditional . . . . incondicional
unconstitutional . . . . inconstitucional
unequal . . . . desigual
unilateral . . . . unilateral
universal. . . . . universal
unofficial . . . . extraoficial
unreal . . . . irreal
unusual . . . . inusual
urinal. . . . . orinal
usual . . . . usual

vegetal. . . . . vegetal
venal . . . . venal
verbal . . . . verbal

vertical. . . . . vertical

vice-presidential . . . . vicepresidencial

viral. . . . . viral

virtual . . . . virtual

visceral . . . . visceral

visual. . . . . visual

vital . . . . vital

vocal . . . . vocal *(also a noun, "vowel")*

vocational. . . . . vocacional

zonal . . . . zonal

Match associated words and/or synonyms.

Una las palabras que están relacionadas o que son sinónimos.

1. animal	contrato
2. personal	gato
3. artificial	sintético
4. crucial	perfecto
5. ideal	importante
6. legal	privado
7. final	terminar

Listen to and read the story. Answer the following questions in complete sentences.

Escuche y lea el cuento. Responda las siguientes preguntas, usando oraciones completas.

(This chapter presents the first story of the travels of Juan and Angélica. Every chapter will feature a new story about these two young Spaniards traveling through Spain. Please listen to and read each story carefully before answering the questions that follow.)

> **Juan y Angélica son dos jóvenes de Bilbao; ellos quieren hacer un viaje** (take a trip)**. Hay un problema—Juan quiere hacer un viaje <u>internacional</u> y Angélica quiere hacer un viaje <u>nacional</u>. Juan dice, "Pero Angélica, tu idea no es <u>original</u>". Angélica dice, "¡Vamos, Juan, no ahora** (not now)**!" Al final, Angélica gana; Juan decide que no es <u>esencial</u> hacer un viaje <u>internacional</u> ahora. Angélica tiene algunas ideas <u>generales</u> para su itinerario. Juan dice, "No quiero visitar a tu tío en**

Córdoba. ¡Él es demasiado <u>formal</u> y <u>tradicional</u>!" Angélica
dice, **"Veremos...**(we'll see)**".**

1. ¿De dónde son Juan y Angélica?

2. ¿Qué tipo de viaje quiere hacer Juan?

3. ¿Qué tipo de viaje quiere hacer Angélica?

4. ¿Qué dice Juan de la idea de Angélica?

5. ¿Según Juan (according to Juan), cómo es el tío de Angélica?

Chapter 2

Many English words ending in "–ance" correspond to "–ancia" in Spanish.

Spanish words ending in "–ancia" are usually feminine nouns. For example,

distance = *la distancia*

All words and phrases in **bold** *are on* **Track 2** *of the accompanying audio.*

ENGLISH. . . . . . . SPANISH

abundance . . . . abundancia
ambulance . . . . **ambulancia**
arrogance. . . . . **arrogancia**
    "Nobody likes arrogance." . . . **"A nadie le gusta la arrogancia".**
assistance. . . . . asistencia

circumstance. . . . . circunstancia
clairvoyance. . . . . clarividencia
concordance. . . . . concordancia
consonance . . . . consonancia
constance. . . . . constancia

discordance . . . . discordancia
dissonance . . . . disonancia
distance . . . . **distancia**

elegance. . . . . **elegancia**
extravagance . . . . extravagancia
exuberance. . . . . exuberancia

flagrance . . . . flagrancia

fragrance . . . . fragancia
France . . . . Francia

ignorance. . . . . ignorancia
importance . . . . **importancia**
    "What is the importance?" . . . **"¿Cuál es la importancia?"**
inobservance . . . . inobservancia
insignificance . . . . insignificancia
instance . . . . instancia
intemperance . . . . intemperancia
intolerance . . . . **intolerancia**
irrelevance . . . . irrelevancia

militance . . . . militancia

observance. . . . . observancia

perseverance . . . . **perseverancia**
    "Perseverance is important." . . . **"La perseverancia es importante".**
predominance. . . . . predominancia
preponderance . . . . preponderancia
protuberance . . . . protuberancia

redundance . . . . redundancia
relevance . . . . relevancia
repugnance . . . . repugnancia
resistance . . . . resistencia
resonance. . . . . resonancia

substance . . . . **substancia**

temperance. . . . . temperancia
tolerance . . . . **tolerancia**

variance. . . . . variancia
vigilance . . . . vigilancia

Una las palabras que están relacionadas o que son sinónimos.

1. fragancia	hospital
2. distancia	significado
3. perseverancia	soberbia
4. tolerancia	lejos
5. arrogancia	constancia
6. ambulancia	perfume
7. importancia	paciencia

Escuche y lea el cuento. Responda las siguientes preguntas, usando oraciones completas.

Para organizar su viaje, Juan y Angélica hablan de muchas cosas. Juan habla de la <u>importancia</u> de no gastar (spend) **mucho; de hecho, Juan no tiene mucha <u>tolerancia</u> hacia el mundo "chic". El sabe que hay gran <u>distancia</u> que cubrir, y que la <u>perseverancia</u> será necesaria. Angélica también entiende la <u>importancia</u> de no gastar mucho dinero durante el viaje. Ella pide** (asks for) **solamente una cosa: quiere ver un baile profesional** (a professional dance) **en Valencia. Una amiga le dijo que es un espectáculo de una <u>elegancia</u> increíble. Juan dice, "Veremos...".**

1. ¿Juan habla de la importancia de qué cosa?

2. ¿Juan no tiene mucha tolerancia hacia qué?

3. ¿Qué será necesario?

4. ¿Angélica entiende la importancia de no gastar mucho dinero?

5. ¿Cómo responde Juan al pedido (request) de Angélica?

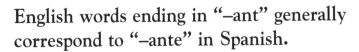

Chapter 3

English words ending in "–ant" generally correspond to "–ante" in Spanish.

Spanish words ending in "–ante" are usually adjectives or nouns. For example,

arrogant (adj.) = *arrogante*
deodorant (n.) = *el desodorante*

ENGLISH. . . . . . . SPANISH

All words and phrases in **bold** are on **Track 3** *of the accompanying audio.*

aberrant. . . . . aberrante
abundant . . . . **abundante**
ambulant . . . . ambulante
antioxidant . . . . antioxidante
arrogant. . . . . **arrogante**
    "He is very arrogant." . . . . . . **"El es muy arrogante"**.
aspirant . . . . aspirante
assailant. . . . . asaltante

brilliant. . . . . brillante

colorant . . . . colorante
commandant. . . . . comandante
communicant. . . . . comunicante
concordant . . . . concordante
consonant. . . . . consonante
constant . . . . **constante** *(also used for "consistent")*
consultant. . . . . consultante
contaminant . . . . contaminante

debutant. . . . . debutante

deodorant	**desodorante**
determinant	determinante
discordant	discordante
disinfectant	desinfectante
dissonant	disonante
distant	distante
dominant	dominante
elegant	**elegante**
elephant	**elefante**
emigrant	emigrante
entrant	entrante
equidistant	equidistante
errant	errante
exorbitant	exorbitante
expectant	expectante
extravagant	extravagante *(also used for "odd")*
exuberant	exuberante
exultant	exultante
flagellant	flagelante
flagrant	flagrante
fluctuant	fluctuante
fumigant	fumigante
gallant	galante
giant	gigante
ignorant	**ignorante**

"What an ignorant question!" . . **"¡Qué pregunta tan ignorante!"**

immigrant	**inmigrante**
implant	implante
important	**importante**
incessant	incesante
inconstant	inconstante
indignant	indignante

infant	infante
informant	informante
inhabitant	habitante
inobservant	inobservante
insignificant	insignificante
instant	**instante**
intolerant	intolerante
irrelevant	irrelevante
irritant	irritante
itinerant	itinerante
lubricant	lubricante
merchant	mercante (only used as an adjective)
migrant	emigrante
militant	militante
mutant	mutante
observant	observante (more commonly "observador")
occupant	**ocupante**
operant	operante
palpitant	palpitante
participant	**participante**
pedant	pedante
piquant	picante
predominant	predominante
preponderant	preponderante
Protestant	protestante
radiant	radiante
rampant	rampante
recalcitrant	recalcitrante
redundant	redundante
refrigerant	refrigerante

relaxant . . . . relajante
relevant . . . . relevante
repugnant. . . . . repugnante
resonant . . . . resonante
restaurant. . . . . **restaurante**
    "That restaurant is cheap." . . . **"Ese restaurante es barato".**

stimulant . . . . **estimulante** *(also used for "stimulating")*
supplicant. . . . . suplicante

tolerant. . . . . tolerante
transplant . . . . transplante
triumphant . . . . **triunfante**

vacant . . . . vacante
variant . . . . variante
vibrant . . . . vibrante
vigilant. . . . . vigilante

3A.

Una las palabras que están relacionadas o que son sinónimos.

1. ignorante	evidente
2. elegante	animal
3. importante	pretencioso
4. elefante	cafetería
5. arrogante	esencial
6. flagrante	desconocedor
7. restaurante	fino

3B.

Escuche y lea el cuento. Responda las siguientes preguntas, usando oraciones completas.

Juan y Angélica deciden ir primero a una ciudad <u>importante</u>: ¡Barcelona! Angélica dice, "Pero Juan, ¿es verdad que la gente (the people) de Barcelona es <u>arrogante</u>?" Juan responde, "¡Pero qué pregunta tan <u>ignorante</u>! No, la gente de Barcelona no es <u>arrogante</u>, su modo de vestir (way of dressing) es muy <u>elegante</u> y saben que la historia de Barcelona es muy <u>importante</u>, pero... son personas muy simpáticas". Juan tiene un amigo, Andrés, que vive en Barcelona y tiene un <u>restaurante</u> que se llama El <u>Elefante</u> Rojo. Apenas llegan (as soon as they arrive) a Barcelona, van a comer al <u>restaurante</u> de Andrés. El les sirve una cena <u>abundante</u>.

1. ¿A qué ciudad van Juan y Angélica?

2. ¿Qué piensa Angélica de la gente de Barcelona?

3. ¿Qué dice Juan del modo de vestir de la gente de Barcelona?

4. ¿Cómo describe Juan la historia de Barcelona?

5. ¿Cómo se llama el restaurante de Andrés?

Chapter 4

Many English words ending in "–ar" have the same ending in Spanish.

Spanish words ending in "–ar" are usually verbs, nouns, or adjectives.
For example,

to arrive (v.) = *llegar*   a dollar (n.) = *un dólar*
spectacular (adj.) = *espectacular*

ENGLISH. . . . . . . SPANISH	

All words and phrases in **bold** *are on* **Track 4** *of the accompanying audio.*

altar. . . . . altar
angular . . . . angular
antinuclear . . . . antinuclear
bipolar. . . . . bipolar
Caesar. . . . . César
cardiovascular . . . . cardiovascular
caviar . . . . caviar
cellular. . . . . **celular**
    "It's a cellular phone." . . . . . . **"Es un teléfono celular"**.
circular. . . . . **circular**
    "It has a circular shape." . . . . **"Tiene una forma circular"**.
collar. . . . . collar *(meaning "necklace")*
curricular . . . . curricular

dollar. . . . . dólar

electronuclear . . . . electronuclear
exemplar . . . . ejemplar
extracurricular. . . . . extracurricular

familiar . . . . familiar

glandular . . . . glandular
globular . . . . globular
granular . . . . granular

insular . . . . insular
intramuscular . . . . intramuscular
irregular . . . . irregular

jugular . . . . yugular

lunar . . . . lunar *(also used for "mole")*

modular . . . . modular
molecular . . . . molecular
multicellular . . . . multicelular
muscular . . . . muscular *(only used for "of the muscle")*

nectar . . . . néctar
nuclear . . . . **nuclear**
   "Nuclear war is terrible." . . . . **"La guerra nuclear es terrible"**.

ocular . . . . ocular

particular . . . . particular
peculiar . . . . peculiar
peninsular . . . . peninsular
perpendicular . . . . perpendicular
polar . . . . **polar**
popular . . . . **popular** *(also used for "of the people")*

radar . . . . radar
rectangular . . . . rectangular
regular . . . . regular *(also used for "less than good")*

scholar . . . . escolar *(meaning "pupil," or "of the school")*

secular . . . . secular

semicircular . . . . semicircular

similar . . . . similar

singular . . . . singular

solar . . . . solar

spectacular . . . . **espectacular**

stellar . . . . estelar

subpolar . . . . subpolar

sugar . . . . azúcar

thermonuclear . . . . termonuclear

triangular . . . . triangular

tubular . . . . tubular

tzar . . . . zar

unicellular . . . . unicelular

unpopular . . . . impopular

vascular . . . . vascular

vehicular . . . . vehicular

vulgar . . . . **vulgar**

Una las palabras que están relacionadas o que son sinónimos.

1. cardiovascular   corazón
2. regular   moneda
3. singular   atómico
4. circular   parecido
5. similar   redondo
6. dólar   constante
7. nuclear   único

Escuche y lea el cuento. Responda las siguientes preguntas, usando oraciones completas.

Mientras están en (while in) **Barcelona, Juan y Angélica van a una lección de italiano con Andrés, el amigo de Juan. Angélica pregunta, "¿Por qué tienes un interés tan <u>particular</u> por el italiano?" Andrés responde, "Porque el italiano es muy <u>popular</u> en Ibiza, y quiero trabajar** (I want to work) **en Ibiza". Durante la lección, el profesor habla de muchos verbos <u>irregulares</u>. Después de la lección, los tres amigos hablan de la diferencia entre** (between) **el <u>singular</u> y el plural en el italiano. El italiano es muy difícil para Angélica. Ella dice, "¡Nada es <u>regular</u>, todo es <u>irregular</u>! ¡Para mí, el italiano es muy difícil!"**

1. ¿Adónde van mientras están en Barcelona?

2. ¿Por qué estudia Andrés italiano?

3. ¿De qué habla el profesor?

4. ¿Los tres amigos hablan de la diferencia entre qué cosas?

5. ¿Angélica piensa que el italiano es muy regular?

Chapter 5

Many English words ending in "–ary" correspond to "–ario" in Spanish.

Spanish words ending in "–ario" are usually masculine nouns or adjectives. For example,

anniversary (n.) = *un aniversario*
ordinary (adj.) = *ordinario*

All words and phrases in **bold** *are on* **Track 5** *of the accompanying audio.*

ENGLISH . . . . SPANISH

actuary . . . . actuario
adversary . . . . adversario
anniversary . . . . **aniversario**
antiquary . . . . anticuario
arbitrary . . . . arbitrario

beneficiary . . . . beneficiario
bestiary . . . . bestiario
binary . . . . binario
breviary . . . . breviario

canary . . . . canario
centenary . . . . centenario
commentary . . . . comentario *(also used for "comment")*
commissary . . . . comisario
complementary . . . . complementario
contrary . . . . **contrario**
corollary . . . . corolario
coronary . . . . coronario
culinary . . . . culinario

depository . . . . depositario
diary . . . . diario *(also used for "newspaper")*
dictionary . . . . **diccionario**
    "He is using the dictionary.". . . **"Él está usando el diccionario"**.
dignitary . . . . dignatario
disciplinary . . . . disciplinario
dispensary . . . . dispensario
divisionary . . . . divisionario
documentary . . . . documentario *(more commonly*
                                "documental," as a noun)

emissary . . . . emisario
estuary . . . . estuario
extraordinary . . . . **extraordinario**

fiduciary . . . . fiduciario
fragmentary . . . . fragmentario
functionary . . . . funcionario
funerary . . . . funerario

glossary . . . . **glosario**

hereditary . . . . hereditario
honorary . . . . honorario

imaginary . . . . **imaginario**
    "He has an imaginary friend." . . . **"Él tiene un amigo imaginario"**.
incendiary . . . . incendiario
interdisciplinary . . . . interdisciplinario
intermediary . . . . intermediario
involuntary . . . . involuntario
itinerary . . . . **itinerario**

lapidary . . . . lapidario
legendary . . . . legendario
literary . . . . literario

-ary/-ario

mercenary	mercenario
monetary	monetario
necessary	**necesario**
notary	notario
obituary	obituario
ordinary	**ordinario**
ovary	ovario
parliamentary	parlamentario
penitentiary	penitenciario
planetary	planetario
plenary	plenario
primary	primario
proprietary	propietario *(also used for "owner")*
questionary	cuestionario *(meaning "questionnaire")*
reactionary	reaccionario
revolutionary	**revolucionario**
rosary	rosario
rudimentary	rudimentario
salary	**salario**

"You have a good salary." . . . **"Tu tienes un buen salario".**

sanctuary	santuario
sanitary	sanitario
secondary	secundario
secretary	**secretario** *(more commonly used in feminine form, "secretaria")*
sedentary	sedentario
sedimentary	sedimentario
seminary	seminario
solitary	**solitario**
stationary	estacionario

subsidiary. . . . . subsidiario
summary . . . . sumario
supplementary. . . . . suplementario

temporary. . . . . temporario
tertiary . . . . terciario
tributary . . . . tributario

unitary . . . . unitario
unnecessary . . . . innecesario
urinary. . . . . urinario

veterinary. . . . . veterinario
visionary . . . . visionario
vocabulary . . . . **vocabulario** *(also used for "dictionary")*
   "Vocabulary is important." . . . **"El vocabulario es importante".**
voluntary . . . . voluntario *(also used for "volunteer")*

Una las palabras que están relacionadas o que son sinónimos.

1. aniversario   palabras
2. salario   ruta
3. necesario   común
4. vocabulario   cumpleaños
5. itinerario   opuesto
6. ordinario   vital
7. contrario   dinero

Escuche y lea el cuento. Responda las siguientes preguntas, usando oraciones completas.

Juan y Angélica tienen un _itinerario_ muy intenso en Barcelona. Para no olvidar (to not forget) **su aventura, Angélica quiere comprar un _diario_ para escribir todo. Un día van a las Ramblas, otro día van a la Sagrada Familia, otro día van a Montserrat. Juan dice, "¡Este ritmo** (this pace) **es _extraordinario_!" Cada noche, Angélica escribe mucho en su _diario_, pero Juan no comprende. El dice, "No es _necesario_ escribir cada detalle** (every detail)—**¡no es un _diccionario_!" Angélica responde, "Al _contrario_, ¡es muy importante escribir cada detalle!"**

1. ¿Cómo es el itinerario de Juan y Angélica en Barcelona?

2. ¿Qué quiere comprar Angélica?

3. ¿Qué escribe Angélica en su diario?

4. ¿Qué dice Juan del ritmo?

5. ¿Según Juan, no es necesario hacer qué cosa?

Chapter 6

Many English words ending in "–ble" have the same ending in Spanish.

Spanish words ending in "–ble" are usually adjectives. For example,

a <u>flexible</u> schedule = *un horario* <u>*flexible*</u>

ENGLISH . . . . SPANISH

All words and phrases in **bold** *are on* **Track 6** *of the accompanying audio.*

abominable . . . . abominable
acceptable . . . . **aceptable**
accessible. . . . . accesible *(also used for "approachable")*
accusable. . . . . acusable
adaptable. . . . . adaptable
adjustable. . . . . ajustable
admirable. . . . . admirable
admissible . . . . admisible
adoptable. . . . . adoptable
adorable . . . . **adorable**
   "The baby is adorable." . . . . **"El bebé es adorable"**.
affable . . . . afable
agreeable. . . . . agradable
alienable . . . . alienable
alterable. . . . . alterable
amiable . . . . amable
amicable . . . . amigable
appealable. . . . . apelable
applicable . . . . aplicable
appreciable . . . . apreciable
arable . . . . arable
audible . . . . audible

biodegradable . . . . biodegradable

cable . . . . cable
calculable. . . . . calculable
cancelable . . . . cancelable
censurable . . . . censurable
classifiable . . . . clasificable
coercible . . . . coercible
collectible. . . . . coleccionable
combinable. . . . . combinable
combustible . . . . combustible
comfortable . . . . confortable *(more commonly "cómodo")*
commemorable . . . . conmemorable
commensurable . . . . conmensurable
communicable. . . . . comunicable
commutable . . . . conmutable
comparable . . . . **comparable**
compatible . . . . compatible
comprehensible. . . . . comprensible
computable. . . . . computable
condemnable . . . . condenable
condensable . . . . condensable
condonable . . . . condonable
confessable. . . . . confesable
conservable . . . . conservable
considerable. . . . . considerable
consolable . . . . consolable
consumable . . . . consumible
contestable . . . . contestable
controllable. . . . . controlable
controvertible . . . . controvertible
convertible . . . . convertible
corruptible . . . . corruptible
countable . . . . contable (also used for "accountant")
credible . . . . **creíble**
   "His story is not credible." . . . **"Su cuento no es creíble"**.

criticizable . . . . criticable
culpable. . . . . culpable
curable. . . . . curable

deductible . . . . deducible
defensible. . . . . defendible
definable . . . . definible
degradable. . . . . degradable
delectable. . . . . deleitable
demonstrable . . . . demostrable
deplorable . . . . deplorable
describable. . . . . descriptible
desirable . . . . deseable
destructible . . . . destructible
determinable. . . . . determinable
detestable. . . . . detestable
digestible . . . . digerible
discussible . . . . discutible
disposable . . . . disponible *(meaning "available")*
disputable. . . . . disputable
distillable . . . . destilable
divisible . . . . **divisible**
dubitable . . . . dudable
durable . . . . durable *(more commonly "duradero")*

eligible. . . . . elegible
eliminable. . . . . eliminable
emendable . . . . enmendable
enviable. . . . . envidiable
estimable . . . . estimable
evaporable. . . . . evaporable
evitable . . . . evitable
excitable . . . . excitable
excludible. . . . . excluible
excusable . . . . **excusable**
expansible . . . . expansible

explicable. . . . . explicable
explorable . . . . explorable
exportable . . . . exportable
extensible . . . . extensible

fallible . . . . falible
favorable . . . . favorable
fermentable . . . . fermentable
filmable . . . . filmable
flexible. . . . . **flexible**
formidable . . . . formidable *(also used for "great,"*
"super")

governable . . . . gobernable

habitable . . . . habitable
honorable. . . . . honorable
horrible . . . . **horrible**

identifiable . . . . identificable
ignoble . . . . innoble
illegible . . . . ilegible
imaginable . . . . imaginable
imitable . . . . imitable
impassible . . . . impasible
impeccable . . . . **impecable**
    "Your Spanish is impeccable." . . . **"Tu español es impecable".**
impenetrable. . . . . impenetrable
imperceptible . . . . imperceptible
impermeable. . . . . impermeable *(also used for "raincoat")*
imperturbable . . . . imperturbable
implacable . . . . implacable
impossible . . . . **imposible**
impressionable . . . . impresionable
improbable. . . . . **improbable**
inaccessible . . . . inaccesible

INSTANT Spanish Vocabulary Builder

inadmissible . . . . inadmisible
inalienable . . . . inalienable
inapplicable . . . . inaplicable
inappreciable . . . . inapreciable *(meaning "invaluable")*
inaudible . . . . inaudible
incalculable . . . . incalculable
incomparable . . . . incomparable
incompatible. . . . . incompatible
incomprehensible . . . . incomprensible
inconsolable . . . . inconsolable
incontestable. . . . . incontestable
incontrovertible . . . . incontrovertible
incorrigible. . . . . incorregible
incorruptible . . . . incorruptible
incredible . . . . **increíble**
incurable . . . . incurable
indefatigable . . . . infatigable
indefinable . . . . indefinible
indelible. . . . . indeleble
indescribable . . . . indescriptible
indestructible. . . . . indestructible
indigestible. . . . . indigerible
indispensable . . . . indispensable
indivisible. . . . . indivisible
ineffable. . . . . inefable
ineligible . . . . inelegible
inestimable . . . . inestimable
inevitable . . . . **inevitable**
inexcusable . . . . inexcusable
inexorable . . . . inexorable
inexplicable . . . . inexplicable
inextricable. . . . . inextricable
infallible. . . . . infalible
inflammable . . . . inflamable
inflexible . . . . **inflexible**
inhabitable . . . . habitable

inimitable . . . . inimitable
inoperable . . . . inoperable
insatiable . . . . insaciable
inscrutable . . . . inescrutable
insensible . . . . insensible *(meaning "insensitive")*
inseparable . . . . inseparable
insoluble. . . . . insoluble
insuperable. . . . . insuperable
intangible . . . . intangible
intelligible. . . . . inteligible
interminable . . . . interminable
interpretable . . . . interpretable
intolerable . . . . intolerable
invariable . . . . invariable
invertible . . . . invertible *(meaning "investable")*
invincible . . . . invencible
inviolable . . . . inviolable
invisible . . . . **invisible**
    "The cover is invisible." . . . . . **"La tapa es invisible".**
invulnerable . . . . invulnerable
irascible . . . . irascible
irreconcilable . . . . irreconciliable
irreducible . . . . irreducible *(also used for "unyielding")*
irrefutable. . . . . irrefutable
irresistible. . . . . irresistible
irresponsible . . . . **irresponsable**
irreversible . . . . irreversible
irrevocable . . . . irrevocable
irrigable . . . . irrigable
irritable . . . . irritable

lamentable . . . . lamentable
laudable. . . . . laudable
legible . . . . legible
limitable . . . . limitable

INSTANT Spanish Vocabulary Builder

malleable . . . . maleable

manageable . . . . manejable

maneuverable . . . . maniobrable

measurable. . . . . mensurable

memorable . . . . memorable

miserable . . . . **miserable** *(also used for "greedy,"*
or "evil")

modifiable . . . . modificable

multipliable. . . . . multiplicable

navigable. . . . . navegable

negotiable . . . . negociable

noble . . . . **noble**

notable. . . . . notable

observable . . . . observable

operable . . . . operable

ostensible . . . . ostensible

palpable. . . . . palpable

pardonable. . . . . perdonable

passable. . . . . **pasable**

"The wine is passable (so-so)." . . . **"El vino está pasable nada más".**

payable . . . . pagable

penetrable . . . . penetrable

perceptible . . . . perceptible

perfectible . . . . perfectible

permeable . . . . permeable

permissible . . . . permisible

persuadable . . . . persuasible

placable. . . . . aplacable

plausible . . . . plausible

ponderable. . . . . ponderable

possible . . . . **posible**

potable . . . . potable

preferable. . . . . preferible

presentable. . . . . presentable

probable . . . . **probable**

producible . . . . producible

programmable . . . . programable

provable. . . . . probable

publishable. . . . . publicable

qualifiable . . . . calificable

quantifiable . . . . cuantificable

realizable. . . . . realizable

recommendable . . . . recomendable

reconcilable . . . . reconciliable

recyclable. . . . . reciclable

reducible . . . . reducible

reformable . . . . reformable

refutable. . . . . refutable

renewable . . . . renovable

repairable . . . . **reparable**

repeatable . . . . repetible

replicable. . . . . replicable

reprehensible . . . . reprensible

representable . . . . representable

resistible. . . . . resistible

respectable. . . . . **respetable**

   "She's a respectable lady." . . . **"Es una señora respetable"**.

responsible. . . . . **responsable**

restorable. . . . . restaurable

retractable . . . . retractable

reversible . . . . reversible

revocable . . . . revocable

savable . . . . salvable

sensible . . . . sensible *(meaning "sensitive")*

separable. . . . . separable

sociable . . . . sociable

soluble . . . . soluble
stable . . . . **estable** *(only an adjective; "horse stable" is "establo")*
superable . . . . superable
susceptible . . . . susceptible

tangible . . . . tangible
terminable . . . . terminable
terrible . . . . terrible
tolerable . . . . tolerable
touchable . . . . tocable
transferable . . . . transferible
transformable . . . . transformable

unacceptable . . . . inaceptable
unadaptable . . . . inadaptable
unalterable . . . . inalterable
unclassifiable . . . . inclasificable
uncontrollable . . . . incontrolable
undesirable . . . . indeseable
undeterminable . . . . indeterminable
undisputable . . . . indisputable
unimaginable . . . . inimaginable
unintelligible . . . . ininteligible
unsociable . . . . insociable
unstable . . . . inestable
untouchable . . . . intocable
utilizable . . . . utilizable

variable . . . . **variable**
venerable . . . . venerable
verifiable . . . . verificable
viable . . . . viable
visible . . . . **visible**
vulnerable . . . . vulnerable

Una las palabras que están relacionadas o que son sinónimos.

1. flexible	rígido
2. terrible	bonito
3. probable	seguro
4. estable	posible
5. inflexible	infeliz
6. miserable	elástico
7. adorable	horrible

Escuche y lea el cuento. Responda las siguientes preguntas, usando oraciones completas.

Después de unos días en Barcelona, Juan y Angélica toman el tren a Valencia. Durante el viaje en tren tienen una pelea (an argument). **Angélica le dice a Juan, "¡Tú eres muy <u>irresponsable</u>! ¡No reservaste** (you didn't reserve) **los asientos para el baile!" Juan responde, "¡Tú eres <u>inflexible</u>, podemos ir en otra ocasión; es muy <u>probable</u> que regresemos a Valencia algún día!" Angélica dice, "¡Eres <u>imposible</u>! ¡Es bastante <u>improbable</u> que regresemos a Valencia!" Al final Juan pide disculpas** (apologizes) **y dice que será mucho mas <u>responsable</u> durante el resto del viaje. Angélica pregunta si será <u>posible</u> comprar los boletos para el baile en Valencia. Juan responde, "Veremos…".**

1. ¿Adónde van después de Barcelona?

-ble/-ble

2. ¿Qué piensa Angélica de Juan?

3. ¿Qué dice Juan de Angélica?

4. ¿Angélica piensa que es probable que regresen a Valencia algún día?

5. ¿Qué pregunta Angélica al final?

Chapter 7

English words ending in "–ct" often correspond to "–cto" in Spanish.

Spanish words ending in "–cto" are usually masculine nouns or adjectives. For example,

contact (n.) = *un contacto*
direct (adj.) = *directo*

ENGLISH . . . . SPANISH	

All words and phrases in **bold** *are on* **Track 7** *of the accompanying audio.*

abstract	abstracto
act	acto
addict	adicto
adjunct	adjunto
affect	afecto
aqueduct	acueducto
architect	arquitecto
artifact	artefacto
aspect	**aspecto**
circumspect	circunspecto
compact	compacto
conflict	conflicto
contact	**contacto**
contract	**contrato**

"The new contract is better." . . . **"El contrato nuevo es mejor"**.

convict	convicto
correct	**correcto**

defect.	defecto
defunct.	difunto
derelict.	derelicto
dialect	**dialecto**
direct	**directo**
"It's a direct flight."	**"Es un vuelo directo".**
distinct	distinto *(meaning "different")*
district	distrito
edict	edicto
effect	efecto
exact	exacto
extinct	extinto
extract	extracto
impact	impacto
imperfect	imperfecto
incorrect.	**incorrecto**
"The answer is incorrect." . . .	**"La respuesta es incorrecta".**
indirect.	**indirecto**
indistinct.	indistinto
inexact.	inexacto
insect.	insecto
instinct	instinto
intact	intacto
intellect.	intelecto
object	objeto
pact.	pacto
perfect	perfecto
prefect	prefecto
product	producto
project	proyecto
prospect	prospecto

select . . . . selecto *(only an adjective)*

strict. . . . . estricto

succinct . . . . sucinto

tact . . . . tacto

verdict . . . . veredicto

viaduct. . . . . viaducto

7A.

Una las palabras que están relacionadas o que son sinónimos.

1. correcto	ideal
2. perfecto	bien
3. incorrecto	parte
4. dialecto	mosca
5. acto	idioma
6. aspecto	mal
7. insecto	teatro

7B.

Escuche y lea el cuento. Responda las siguientes preguntas, usando oraciones completas.

Después de bajar del tren <u>directo</u> de Barcelona a Valencia, Angélica pregunta si éste es el lugar <u>correcto</u> porque ella no comprende nada. Ella sabe que el español hablado (spoken Spanish) **no es siempre <u>perfecto</u>, ¡pero no comprende este acento ni un poquito! Juan dice, "No te preocupes** (don't worry)**, tengo un buen <u>contacto</u> aquí en Valencia; se llama Alfonso, y él nos ayudará a conseguir los boletos". Después de unos minutos en la estación, Alfonso viene a recogerlos** (pick them up)**. "Tiene <u>aspecto</u> de ser muy buena persona", dice Angélica. Alfonso es muy gracioso y tiene mucho respeto por su amigo Juan y su novia Angélica. Después de una buena cena en casa de Alfonso—la salsa estuvo <u>perfecta</u>—Angélica le pregunta si sabe algo sobre el baile en el centro. Alfonso responde, "Veremos…".**

INSTANT Spanish Vocabulary Builder

1. ¿Qué tipo de tren tomaron de Barcelona?

2. ¿Por qué piensa Angélica que no es el lugar correcto?

3. ¿Por qué no comprende Angélica el español en Valencia?

4. ¿Cómo se llama el contacto de Juan en Valencia?

5. ¿Cómo estuvo la salsa de Alfonso?

Chapter 8

English words ending in "–ence" often correspond to "–encia" in Spanish.

Spanish words ending in "–encia" are usually feminine nouns. For example,

a difference = *una diferencia*

<table>
<tr><td>ENGLISH. . . . . . . SPANISH</td></tr>
</table>

All words and phrases in **bold** *are on* **Track 8** *of the accompanying audio.*

ENGLISH	SPANISH
absence	**ausencia**
abstinence	abstinencia
adherence	adherencia
adolescence	adolescencia
ambivalence	ambivalencia
antiviolence	antiviolencia
audience	audiencia *(more commonly "público")*
belligerence	beligerancia
beneficence	beneficencia
benevolence	benevolencia
cadence	cadencia
circumference	circunferencia
coexistence	coexistencia
coherence	coherencia
coincidence	**coincidencia**
"What a coincidence!"	**"¡Qué coincidencia!"**
competence	competencia *(also used for "competition")*
complacence	complacencia
condescendence	condescendencia

condolence . . . . condolencia
conference . . . . **conferencia**
confidence . . . . confidencia *(meaning "secret/private information")*

confluence . . . . confluencia
congruence . . . . congruencia
conscience . . . . conciencia
consequence . . . . **consecuencia**
consistence . . . . consistencia
continence . . . . continencia
convalescence . . . . convalecencia
convenience . . . . conveniencia
convergence . . . . convergencia
corpulence . . . . corpulencia
correspondence . . . . correspondencia

decadence . . . . decadencia
deference . . . . deferencia
dependence . . . . dependencia
difference . . . . **diferencia**
  "The difference is notable." . . . **"La diferencia es notable".**
diligence . . . . diligencia
disobedience . . . . desobediencia
dissidence . . . . disidencia
divergence . . . . divergencia

effervescence . . . . efervescencia
eloquence . . . . elocuencia
emergence . . . . emergencia *(meaning "emergency")*
eminence . . . . eminencia
equivalence . . . . equivalencia
essence . . . . esencia
evidence . . . . evidencia
excellence . . . . excelencia
existence . . . . existencia
experience . . . . **experiencia**

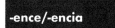

fluorescence . . . . fluorescencia
frequence . . . . frecuencia *(also used for "frequency")*

imminence . . . . inminencia
impatience . . . . **impaciencia**
impermanence . . . . impermanencia
impertinence . . . . impertinencia
impotence . . . . impotencia
imprudence . . . . imprudencia
impudence . . . . impudencia
incandescence . . . . incandescencia
incidence . . . . incidencia *(also used for "impact," "effect")*
incoherence . . . . incoherencia
incompetence . . . . incompetencia
incongruence . . . . incongruencia
inconsequence . . . . inconsecuencia
inconsistence . . . . inconsistencia
incontinence . . . . incontinencia
inconvenience . . . . inconveniencia
independence . . . . independencia
indifference . . . . **indiferencia**
"I hate indifference." . . . . **"Odio la indiferencia".**
indigence . . . . indigencia
indolence . . . . indolencia
indulgence . . . . indulgencia
inexistence . . . . inexistencia
inexperience . . . . inexperiencia
inference . . . . inferencia
influence . . . . **influencia**
infrequence . . . . infrecuencia
innocence . . . . **inocencia**
insistence . . . . insistencia
insolence . . . . insolencia
intelligence . . . . **inteligencia**

interdependence . . . . interdependencia
interference. . . . . interferencia
intransigence . . . . intransigencia
irreverence . . . . irreverencia

jurisprudence . . . . jurisprudencia

license . . . . licencia *(also used for "permit")*
luminescence . . . . luminiscencia

magnificence . . . . magnificencia
malevolence . . . . malevolencia
munificence . . . . munificencia

negligence . . . . negligencia
neuroscience. . . . . neurociencia

obedience . . . . obediencia
obsolescence . . . . obsolescencia
occurrence . . . . ocurrencia *(also used for*
"bright idea")
omnipotence. . . . . omnipotencia
omnipresence . . . . omnipresencia
opulence . . . . opulencia

patience. . . . . **paciencia**
"Pedro has little patience.". . . **"Pedro tiene poca paciencia"**.
penitence . . . . penitencia
permanence . . . . permanencia
persistence . . . . persistencia
pertinence . . . . pertinencia
pestilence. . . . . pestilencia
precedence. . . . . precedencia
preeminence. . . . . preeminencia
preexistence . . . . preexistencia
preference . . . . **preferencia**

INSTANT Spanish Vocabulary Builder

presence . . . . **presencia**
prominence . . . . prominencia
providence . . . . providencia
prudence . . . . prudencia

quintessence . . . . quintaesencia

reference . . . . referencia
reminiscence . . . . reminiscencia
residence . . . . **residencia**
reticence . . . . reticencia
reverence . . . . reverencia

science . . . . **ciencia**
sentence . . . . sentencia *(meaning "ruling")*
sequence . . . . **secuencia**
somnolence . . . . somnolencia
subsistence . . . . subsistencia
succulence . . . . suculencia

teleconference . . . . teleconferencia
transcendence . . . . transcendencia
transference . . . . transferencia
transparence . . . . trasparencia
truculence . . . . truculencia
turbulence . . . . turbulencia

vehemence . . . . vehemencia
videoconference . . . . videoconferencia
violence . . . . **violencia**
virulence . . . . virulencia

Una las palabras que están relacionadas o que son sinónimos.

1. paciencia	prueba
2. conferencia	reunión
3. residencia	guerra
4. diferencia	liberación
5. violencia	casa
6. evidencia	esperar
7. independencia	distincion

Escuche y lea el cuento. Responda las siguientes preguntas, usando oraciones completas.

El día después, Alfonso le dice a Angélica, "¡Qué coincidencia! Mi novia y yo vamos al baile mañana por la noche, ¿queréis venir (do you two want to come) con nosotros?" El día después Angélica está muy contenta y le dice a Juan: "¿Ves? La persistencia y diligencia ayudan". Juan está muy contento por la felicidad de Angélica y piensa que será una buena experiencia. Desafortunadamente (unfortunately) Juan no tiene ni mucha paciencia ni mucho interés por el baile. Trata de esconder (he tries to hide) su indiferencia. Juan le dice a Angélica, "Lo siento por mi impaciencia, pero... ¡el baile está terrible!" Después de dos días con Alfonso en Valencia, Juan y Angélica van a Ibiza.

1. ¿Qué dice Alfonso del baile?

2. Según Angélica, ¿qué cosas ayudan?

3. ¿Qué expectativas (expectations) tiene Juan hacia el baile?

4. ¿A Juan le causa pasión o indiferencia el baile?

5. ¿Por qué pide disculpas (apologizes) Juan?

Chapter 9

English words ending in "–ent" often correspond to "–ente" in Spanish (excluding words ending in "–ment," which is a separate pattern).

Spanish words ending in "–ente" are usually adjectives or nouns. For example,

innocent (adj.) = *inocente*
client (n.) = *un/una cliente*

ENGLISH. . . . . . . SPANISH	

All words and phrases in **bold** *are on* **Track 9** *of the accompanying audio.*

absent . . . . ausente
absorbent . . . . absorbente
accident . . . . accidente
adherent . . . . adherente
adjacent . . . . adyacente
adolescent . . . . adolescente
agent . . . . **agente**
ambient . . . . ambiente *(meaning "environment")*
ambivalent . . . . ambivalente
antecedent . . . . antecedente
apparent . . . . aparente
ardent . . . . ardiente
astringent . . . . astringente

benevolent . . . . benevolente

client . . . . **cliente**
    "Miguel has no clients." . . . . . **"Miguel no tiene clientes".**
coefficient . . . . coeficiente

coexistent . . . . coexistente
coherent . . . . coherente
competent . . . . **competente**
complacent . . . . complaciente *(meaning "willing*
to please")
component . . . . componente
concupiscent . . . . concupiscente
concurrent . . . . concurrente
confident . . . . confidente *(meaning "a confidant")*
congruent . . . . congruente
consequent . . . . consiguiente
consistent . . . . consistente *(meaning "firm," "solid")*
constituent . . . . constituyente
continent . . . . **continente**
contingent . . . . contingente
convalescent . . . . convalesciente
convenient . . . . conveniente
convergent . . . . convergente
copresident . . . . copresidente
correspondent . . . . correspondiente
crescent . . . . creciente
current . . . . corriente

decadent . . . . decadente
decent . . . . decente
deficient . . . . deficiente
delinquent . . . . delincuente
dependent . . . . dependiente *(also used for "employee")*
descendent . . . . descendiente
detergent . . . . detergente
different . . . . **diferente**
"I want something different." . . . . **"Quiero algo diferente".**
diligent . . . . diligente
disobedient . . . . desobediente
dissident . . . . disidente
dissolvent . . . . disolvente

divergent . . . . divergente

effervescent . . . . efervescente
efficient . . . . eficiente
eloquent. . . . . elocuente
emergent . . . . emergente
eminent . . . . eminente
equivalent. . . . . equivalente
evanescent . . . . evanescente
evident. . . . . evidente
excellent. . . . . excelente
exigent. . . . . exigente
existent. . . . . existente
exponent . . . . exponente

fervent . . . . ferviente
fluorescent . . . . fluorescente
frequent . . . . **frecuente**

imminent . . . . inminente
impatient . . . . **impaciente**
    "Carlos is very impatient." . . . . **"Carlos es muy impaciente".**
impertinent . . . . impertinente
impotent. . . . . impotente
imprudent. . . . . imprudente
impudent . . . . impudente
incandescent. . . . . incandescente
incident . . . . incidente
incipient. . . . . incipiente
incoherent . . . . incoherente
incompetent . . . . incompetente
incongruent. . . . . incongruente
inconsistent. . . . . inconsistente *(meaning "flimsy")*
incontinent . . . . incontinente
inconvenient . . . . inconveniente *(also used for*
                                  "inconvenience")

indecent . . . . indecente
independent . . . . independiente
indifferent. . . . . **indiferente**
indigent . . . . indigente
indolent . . . . indolente
indulgent . . . . indulgente
inefficient . . . . ineficiente
inexistent . . . . inexistente
infrequent. . . . . infrecuente
ingredient. . . . . **ingrediente**
inherent . . . . inherente
innocent . . . . **inocente**
insistent . . . . insistente
insolent . . . . insolente
insolvent. . . . . insolvente
insufficient . . . . insuficiente
insurgent . . . . insurgente
intelligent . . . . **inteligente**

    "Pablo is very intelligent." . . . **"Pablo es muy inteligente"**.

interdependent . . . . interdependiente
intermittent . . . . intermitente
intransigent. . . . . intransigente
iridescent . . . . iridiscente
irreverent . . . . irreverente

latent . . . . latente
luminescent. . . . . luminiscente

magnificent. . . . . magnificente *(more commonly*
                            "magnífico")
munificent. . . . . munificente

nascent . . . . naciente
negligent . . . . negligente
nutrient. . . . . nutriente

obedient. . . . . obediente
occident . . . . occidente
omnipotent . . . . omnipotente
omnipresent . . . . omnipresente
omniscient . . . . omnisciente
orient. . . . . oriente

parent . . . . pariente *(meaning "a relative")*
patent . . . . patente
patient . . . . **paciente**
penitent . . . . penitente
permanent . . . . **permanente**
persistent . . . . persistente
pertinent. . . . . pertinente
pestilent . . . . pestilente
phosphorescent. . . . . fosforescente
potent . . . . potente
precedent. . . . . precedente
preeminent . . . . preeminente
preexistent . . . . preexistente
present. . . . . **presente**
president . . . . **presidente**
  "There's a new president." . . . **"Hay un presidente nuevo".**
prominent. . . . . prominente

quotient . . . . cociente

recent. . . . . reciente
recipient. . . . . recipiente *(also used for "container,"
                                                "bowl")*
recurrent. . . . . recurrente
redolent . . . . redolente
repellent. . . . . repelente
resident . . . . **residente**
reticent. . . . . reticente
reverent . . . . reverente

serpent. . . . . serpiente
silent . . . . silente *(more commonly "silencioso")*
solvent . . . . solvente
strident. . . . . estridente
subsequent . . . . subsiguiente
sufficient. . . . . suficiente
superintendent. . . . . superintendente

tangent . . . . **tangente**
torrent . . . . torrente
transcendent. . . . . trascendente
transparent. . . . . transparente
trident . . . . tridente

urgent . . . . **urgente**

vehement . . . . vehemente
vice president . . . . vicepresidente

Una las palabras que están relacionadas o que son sinónimos.

1. permanente   obvio
2. reciente   jefe
3. diferente   actual
4. presidente   nuevo
5. evidente   habitante
6. residente   fijo
7. presente   distinto

Escuche y lea el cuento. Responda las siguientes preguntas, usando oraciones completas.

Cuando llegan a Ibiza, Angélica llama a su madre y recibe un mensaje <u>urgente</u>: debe visitar a su primo (her cousin) **en Ibiza. Su primo Diego es el <u>presidente</u> de una compañía médica. Juan le dice, "Describe a tu primo, ¿cómo es?" Angélica responde, "Bueno, mi primo es... <u>diferente</u>... es un médico muy <u>competente</u> y muy, muy <u>inteligente</u>, pero es un poco extraño** (a bit strange)**". Juan quiere saber por qué es tan "<u>diferente</u>". Angélica le dice, "Ya verás** (you'll see)**, él piensa que todos somos médicos <u>residentes</u>". Juan dice, "Está bien, veremos...".**

1. ¿Qué tipo de mensaje recibe Angélica?

2. ¿Diego es el presidente de qué?

3. ¿Qué dice Angélica de su primo?

4. Según Angélica, ¿es Diego inteligente?

5. ¿Qué dice Juan al final?

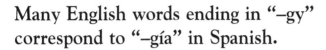

Chapter 10

Many English words ending in "–gy" correspond to "–gía" in Spanish.

Spanish words ending in "–gía" are usually feminine nouns. For example,

the energy = *la energía*

ENGLISH . . . . SPANISH

All words and phrases in **bold** *are on* **Track 10** *of the accompanying audio.*

allergy . . . . **alergia**
    "Ana has a few allergies." . . . **"Ana tiene unas alergias"**.
analogy . . . . analogía
anesthesiology . . . . anestesiología
anthology . . . . antología
anthropology . . . . antropología
archaeology . . . . arqueología
astrology . . . . astrología
audiology . . . . audiología

biology . . . . **biología**
biotechnology . . . . biotecnología

cardiology . . . . cardiología
chronology . . . . **cronología**
climatology . . . . climatología
cosmetology . . . . cosmetología
cosmology . . . . cosmología
criminology . . . . criminología
cryptology . . . . criptología

dermatology . . . . dermatología

ecology . . . . ecología
Egyptology . . . . egiptología
elegy . . . . elegía
endocrinology . . . . endocrinología
energy . . . . **energía**
    "We need energy." . . . . **"Necesitamos energía".**
epidemiology . . . . epidemiología
ethnology . . . . etnología
etymology. . . . . etimología

gastroenterology . . . . gastroenterología
genealogy . . . . genealogía
geology . . . . **geología**
gynecology. . . . . ginecología

hydrology. . . . . hidrología

ideology . . . . **ideología**

liturgy . . . . liturgia

meteorology . . . . **meteorología**
methodology. . . . . metodología
microbiology. . . . . microbiología
mineralogy . . . . mineralogía
morphology . . . . morfología
musicology . . . . musicología
mythology . . . . **mitología**

neurobiology . . . . neurobiología
neurology. . . . . neurología
numerology . . . . numerología

oncology . . . . oncología
ontology. . . . . ontología
ophthalmology . . . . oftalmología

orgy. . . . . orgía

paleontology. . . . . paleontología
parapsychology . . . . parasicología
pathology. . . . . patología
pedagogy. . . . . pedagogía
pharmacology. . . . . farmacología
philology . . . . filología
phonology . . . . fonología
phraseology . . . . fraseología
physiology . . . . fisiología
proctology . . . . proctología
psychology . . . . **psicología**
     "She studies psychology." . . . **"Ella estudia psicología"**.

radiology . . . . **radiología**
rheumatology . . . . reumatología

seismology . . . . sismología
sociology . . . . sociología
strategy . . . . **estrategia**
     "They have a strategy." . . . . . **"Ellos tienen una estrategia"**.
synergy . . . . sinergia

technology . . . . **tecnología**
terminology. . . . . terminología
theology. . . . . teología
topology. . . . . topología
toxicology. . . . . toxicología
trilogy . . . . **trilogía**
typology. . . . . tipología

urology . . . . urología

zoology . . . . zoología

Una las palabras que están relacionadas o que son sinónimos.

1. biología	historia
2. radiología	vida
3. tecnología	tres
4. trilogía	plan
5. estrategia	computadora
6. cronología	rayos X
7. geología	tierra

Escuche y lea el cuento. Responda las siguientes preguntas, usando oraciones completas.

A las nueve de la mañana Juan y Angélica van a la casa de Diego. El vive en San Miguel y es un hombre muy simpático y tiene mucha energía. Dice de pronto (suddenly), **"Hola muchachos, ¿tienen alguna alergia al café?"** Los muchachos dicen que no y todos toman un café juntos. Diego empieza en seguida (right away) a **hablar de nuevas tecnologías médicas y le pregunta a Juan si estudia radiología. Juan dice que nunca ha estudiado** (he never studied) **radiología pero sí hizo un año de biología. Diego le pregunta a Angélica si estudia psicología. Cuando ella dice que no, Diego dice, "Entonces, ¿estudias meteorología?" Angélica mira a Juan; él entiende rapidamente lo que significa "diferente".**

1. ¿Diego es perezoso (lazy) o tiene mucha energía?

2. ¿Los muchachos tienen alergia al café?

3. ¿De qué habla Diego?

4. ¿Estudia Juan radiología?

5. ¿Estudia Angélica psicología?

Chapter 11

English words ending in "–ic" often correspond to "–ico" in Spanish.

Spanish words ending in "–ico" are usually adjectives. For example,

a <u>drastic</u> situation = *una situación <u>drastica</u>*

ENGLISH. . . . . . . SPANISH

All words and phrases in **bold** *are on* **Track 11** *of the accompanying audio.*

academic	académico
acoustic	acústico
acrobatic	acrobático
acrylic	acrílico
Adriatic	Adriático
aerobic	aeróbico
aerodynamic	aerodinámico
aeronautic	aeronáutico
aesthetic	estético
agnostic	agnóstico
alcoholic	**alcohólico**
"It's an alcoholic drink."	**"Es un trago alcohólico".**
algebraic	algebraico
allergic	**alérgico**
alphabetic	alfabético
altruistic	altruístico *(more commonly "altruista")*
anabolic	anabólico
analytic	analítico
anarchic	anárquico
anatomic	anatómico
anemic	anémico

anesthetic . . . . anestésico

angelic. . . . . angélico *(more commonly "angelical")*

anorexic. . . . . anoréxico

antagonistic . . . . antagónico

antarctic. . . . . antártico

antibiotic . . . . antibiótico

anticlimactic . . . . anticlimático

antidemocratic . . . . antidemocrático

anti-Semitic . . . . antisemítico

antiseptic . . . . antiséptico

apologetic . . . . apologético

aquatic. . . . . acuático

Arabic . . . . arábico *(more commonly árabe)*

arctic . . . . ártico

archaic. . . . . arcaico

aristocratic . . . . aristocrático

arithmetic . . . . aritmético *(only an adjective)*

aromatic. . . . . aromático

artistic . . . . **artístico**

arthritic . . . . artrítico

asthmatic . . . . asmático

astronomic . . . . astronómico

asymmetric . . . . asimétrico

atheistic . . . . ateístico

athletic . . . . **atlético**

Atlantic . . . . Atlántico

atmospheric . . . . atmosférico

atomic . . . . atómico

attic . . . . ático

authentic . . . . **auténtico**

    "The food is authentic." . . . . . **"La comida es auténtica".**

autistic . . . . autístico

autobiographic . . . . autobiográfico

autocratic . . . . autocrático

automatic . . . . automático

ballistic . . . . balístico

INSTANT Spanish Vocabulary Builder

balsamic . . . . balsámico
Baltic . . . . báltico
barbaric . . . . barbárico *(more commonly "bárbaro")*
barometric . . . . barométrico
basic . . . . básico
biographic . . . . biográfico
bombastic . . . . bombástico
botanic . . . . botánico
bubonic . . . . bubónico
bucolic . . . . bucólico
bureaucratic . . . . burocrático

calisthenic . . . . calisténico
catastrophic . . . . catastrófico
catatonic . . . . catatónico
cathartic . . . . catártico
Catholic . . . . **católico**
caustic . . . . cáustico
Celtic . . . . céltico
ceramic . . . . cerámico *(only an adjective,*
                                       noun is "cerámica")
chaotic . . . . caótico
characteristic . . . . característico
charismatic . . . . carismático
choleric . . . . colérico
chronic . . . . **crónico**
chronologic . . . . cronológico
citric . . . . cítrico
civic . . . . cívico
classic . . . . **clásico**
   "It's a classic book." . . . . **"Es un libro clásico".**
climatic . . . . climático
colic . . . . cólico
comic . . . . cómico *(also used for "comedian")*
concentric . . . . concéntrico
cosmetic . . . . cosmético

cosmic . . . . cósmico
critic . . . . crítico *(also used for "critical")*
cryptic . . . . críptico
cubic . . . . cúbico
cylindric . . . . cilíndrico
cynic . . . . cínico

democratic . . . . **democrático**
demographic . . . . demográfico
despotic . . . . despótico
diabetic . . . . diabético
diabolic . . . . diabólico
diagnostic. . . . . diagnóstico
didactic . . . . didáctico
dietetic. . . . . dietético
diplomatic . . . . diplomático
diuretic. . . . . diurético
dogmatic . . . . dogmático
domestic. . . . . **doméstico** *(for politics and flights,*
use "nacional")
doric . . . . dórico
dramatic. . . . . dramático
drastic . . . . **drástico**
"The situation is not drastic.". . . . **"La situación no es drástica"**.
dynamic. . . . . dinámico
dyslexic . . . . disléxico

eccentric. . . . . excéntrico
ecclesiastic . . . . eclesiástico
eclectic. . . . . ecléctico
economic . . . . económico *(also used for "inexpensive")*
ecstatic. . . . . extático
egocentric . . . . egocéntrico
elastic . . . . elástico
electric. . . . . eléctrico
electromagnetic. . . . . electromagnético

INSTANT Spanish Vocabulary Builder

electronic	**electrónico**
emblematic	emblemático
emphatic	enfático
energetic	enérgico
enigmatic	enigmático
enthusiastic	entusiástico
epic	épico
epileptic	epiléptico
erotic	erótico
erratic	errático
esoteric	esotérico
ethic	ético
ethnic	étnico
ethnocentric	etnocéntrico
euphoric	eufórico
evangelic	evangélico
exotic	**exótico**
fanatic	fanático
fantastic	**fantástico**
folic	fólico
folkloric	folclórico
forensic	forénsico
frenetic	frenético
galactic	galáctico
gastric	gástrico
gastronomic	gastrónomico
generic	genérico
genetic	genético
geographic	geográfico
geologic	geológico
geometric	geométrico
geriatric	geriátrico
Germanic	germánico
gothic	gótico

graphic . . . . gráfico
gymnastic. . . . . gimnástico

harmonic . . . . armónico
hedonistic. . . . . hedonístico
hegemonic . . . . hegemónico
hemispheric . . . . hemisférico
heretic . . . . herético
heroic . . . . **heroico**
    "It was a heroic action." . . . . **"Fue una acción heroica".**
hieroglyphic . . . . jeroglífico
Hispanic. . . . . hispánico *(more commonly "hispano")*
historic . . . . **histórico**
histrionic. . . . . histriónico
holistic . . . . holístico
homeopathic. . . . . homeopático
Homeric . . . . homérico
hydraulic . . . . hidráulico
hygienic. . . . . higiénico
hyperbolic . . . . hiperbólico
hypnotic. . . . . hipnótico
hypodermic . . . . hipodérmico
hysteric . . . . histérico

ideologic . . . . ideológico
idiomatic . . . . idiomático
idyllic. . . . . idílico
illogic. . . . . ilógico
intrinsic . . . . intrínseco
ionic . . . . iónico
ironic . . . . **irónico**
    "It's an ironic situation." . . . . . **"Es una situación irónica".**
Islamic . . . . islámico
isometric. . . . . isométrico
italic . . . . itálico

Jurassic . . . . Jurásico

kinetic . . . . cinético

laconic. . . . . lacónico
lethargic. . . . . letárgico
linguistic. . . . . lingüístico
lithographic . . . . litográfico
logic . . . . lógico (only an adjective;
                                        noun is "lógica")
logistic. . . . . logístico
lunatic . . . . lunático
lyric . . . . lírico

macroeconomic. . . . . macroeconómico
magic . . . . mágico (only an adjective;
                                        noun is "magia")
magnetic . . . . magnético
mathematic. . . . . matemático
mechanic . . . . mecánico (also used for "mechanical")
medic. . . . . médico (also used for "medical")
melodic . . . . melódico
melodramatic . . . . melodramático
metabolic . . . . metabólico
metallic . . . . metálico
metalinguistic . . . . metalingüístico
metaphoric . . . . metafórico
metaphysic . . . . metafísico
meteoric . . . . meteórico
methodic . . . . metódico
metric. . . . . métrico
microeconomic . . . . microeconómico
microscopic. . . . . microscópico
misanthropic. . . . . misantrópico
mnemonic. . . . . mnémonico
monopolistic . . . . monopolístico

mosaic . . . . mosaico
multiethnic . . . . multiétnico
mystic . . . . místico
mythic . . . . mítico

napoleonic . . . . napoleónico
narcotic . . . . narcótico
neurologic . . . . neurológico
neurotic . . . . neurótico
Nordic . . . . nórdico
nostalgic . . . . **nostálgico**
numeric . . . . numérico

oceanic . . . . oceánico
olympic . . . . olímpico *(for the sporting event,*
use "olimpiadas")
onomatopoeic . . . . onomatopéyico
optic . . . . óptico
organic . . . . orgánico
orgasmic . . . . orgásmico
orthopedic . . . . ortopédico

Pacific . . . . Pacífico
panic . . . . **pánico**
Paleozoic . . . . Paleozoico
panoramic . . . . panorámico
parasitic . . . . parasítico
pathetic . . . . **patético**
pathologic . . . . patológico
patriotic . . . . **patriótico**
"The people are very patriotic." . . . **"El público es muy patriótico".**
pediatric . . . . pediátrico
periodic . . . . periódico *(also used*
for "newspaper")
phallic . . . . fálico
philanthropic . . . . filantrópico

philosophic . . . . filosófico
phobic . . . . fóbico
phonetic . . . . fonético
photogenic . . . . fotogénico
photographic . . . . fotográfico
plastic . . . . plástico
platonic . . . . platónico
pneumatic . . . . pneumático *(also used for "tire")*
poetic . . . . **poético**
polemic . . . . polémico
pornographic . . . . pornográfico
pragmatic . . . . pragmático
prehistoric . . . . prehistórico
problematic . . . . problemático
prolific . . . . prolífico
prophetic . . . . profético
prophylactic . . . . profiláctico
prosaic . . . . prosaico
prosthetic . . . . protésico
psychedelic . . . . psicodélico
psychiatric . . . . psiquiátrico
psychic . . . . psíquico
psychopathic . . . . psicopático
psychotic . . . . psicótico
pubic . . . . púbico
public . . . . público *(also used for "audience")*

rhetoric . . . . retórico
rheumatic . . . . reumático
rhythmic . . . . rítmico
robotic . . . . robótico
romantic . . . . **romántico**
   "It's a romantic city." . . . . **"Es una ciudad romántica"**.
rustic . . . . rústico

sadistic . . . . sádico

sarcastic	**sarcástico**
sardonic	sardónico
satanic	satánico
satiric	satírico
scenic	escénico
schematic	esquemático
schizophrenic	esquizofrénico
scholastic	escolástico
scientific	**científico**
semantic	semántico
semiautomatic	semiautomático
semiotic	semiótico
septic	séptico
skeptic	escéptico
sociolinguistic	sociolingüístico
sonic	sónico
soporific	soporífico
spasmodic	espasmódico
spastic	espástico
specific	**específico**
spheric	esférico
sporadic	esporádico
static	estático
statistic	estadístico
stoic	estoico
strategic	**estratégico**
stylistic	estilístico
subatomic	subatómico
supersonic	supersónico
symbolic	**simbólico**
"It's a symbolic gift."	**"Es un regalo simbólico".**
symmetric	simétrico
symptomatic	sintomático
synthetic	sintético
systematic	sistemático

telegenic . . . . telegénico
telegraphic . . . . telegráfico
telepathic . . . . telepático
telescopic . . . . telescópico
terrific . . . . terrífico *(meaning "terrifying")*
thematic . . . . temático
theoretic . . . . teórico
therapeutic . . . . terapeutico
titanic . . . . titánico
tonic . . . . tónico
topic . . . . tópico
touristic . . . . turístico
toxic . . . . tóxico
traffic . . . . tráfico
tragic . . . . trágico
traumatic . . . . traumático
tropic . . . . trópico

ultrasonic . . . . ultrasónico

volcanic . . . . volcánico

Una las palabras que están relacionadas o que son sinónimos.

1. pragmático	práctico
2. trafico	detalles
3. auténtico	amoroso
4. específico	carros
5. electrónico	intemporal
6. clásico	estéreo
7. romántico	verdadero

Escuche y lea el cuento. Responda las siguientes preguntas, usando oraciones completas.

Después de dos días en Ibiza, Juan y Angélica van a Alicante. Alicante es bellísima, de una belleza <u>clásica</u>. Durante el día (during the day) **van a algunos museos <u>artísticos</u>, y por la noche ven lo <u>mágico</u> que es Alicante. No hay una explicación <u>específica</u>, pero Alicante es una ciudad <u>fantástica</u>. Juan conduce un carro alquilado** (rented car)**, pero hay mucho <u>tráfico</u>. Angélica dice que no es un plan muy <u>estratégico</u>. En Alicante hay siempre mucho <u>tráfico</u> en el verano. Ella dice, "El tren es mejor** (better)**, no es muy <u>romántico</u> pasar las vacaciones dentro de un carro". Juan responde, "Veremos...".**

INSTANT Spanish Vocabulary Builder

1. ¿Cuál es el problema cuando Juan conduce?

2. ¿Por qué dice Angélica, "El tren es mejor"?

3. ¿Qué tipos de museos visitan?

4. ¿Cuándo es mágico Alicante?

5. ¿Qué tipo de ciudad es Alicante?

Chapter 12

Many English words ending in "–ical" correspond to "–ico" in Spanish.

Spanish words ending in "–ico" are usually adjectives. For example,

identical twins = *gemelos idénticos*

ENGLISH. . . . . . . SPANISH	All words and phrases in **bold** are on **Track 12** of the accompanying audio.

acoustical . . . . acústico
aeronautical . . . . aeronáutico
allegorical . . . . alegórico
alphabetical . . . . **alfabético**
    "It's in alphabetical order." . . . **"Está en orden alfabético"**.
analytical . . . . analítico
anarchical . . . . anárquico
anatomical . . . . anatómico
antithetical . . . . antitético
apolitical . . . . apolítico
archaeological . . . . **arqueológico**
astrological. . . . . astrológico
astronomical . . . . astronómico
asymmetrical. . . . . asimétrico
atypical . . . . atípico
autobiographical. . . . . autobiográfico

biblical. . . . . bíblico
bibliographical . . . . bibliográfico
biochemical . . . . bioquímico
biographical . . . . biográfico
biological . . . . **biológico**

botanical . . . . **botánico**

categorical . . . . categórico
chemical. . . . . químico
chronological . . . . cronológico
classical . . . . clásico
clinical . . . . clínico
comical . . . . cómico *(also used for "comedian")*
critical . . . . **crítico** *(also used for "critic")*
cubical. . . . . cúbico
cyclical. . . . . cíclico
cylindrical. . . . . cilíndrico
cynical . . . . **cínico**

demographical . . . . demográfico
diabolical. . . . . diabólico
dialectical. . . . . dialéctico

ecclesiastical. . . . . eclesiástico
ecological. . . . . ecológico
economical. . . . . económico
electrical. . . . . **eléctrico**
elliptical . . . . elíptico
empirical . . . . empírico
ethical . . . . ético
evangelical. . . . . evangélico

fanatical. . . . . fanático

gastronomical . . . . gastronómico
genealogical. . . . . genealógico
geographical . . . . geográfico
geological . . . . geológico
geometrical. . . . . geométrico
grammatical . . . . gramático

hierarchical . . . . jerárquico
historical . . . . histórico
hypothetical . . . . hipotético
hysterical . . . . histérico

identical . . . . **idéntico**
   "They are identical twins." . . . **"Son gemelos idénticos".**
ideological . . . . ideológico
illogical . . . . ilógico
impractical . . . . impráctico
ironical. . . . . irónico
lexical . . . . léxico *(meaning "lexicon,"*
                                    "vocabulary")

logical . . . . **lógico**
logistical. . . . . logístico
lyrical. . . . . lírico

magical . . . . **mágico**
mathematical . . . . matemático
mechanical. . . . . mecánico *(also used for "mechanic")*
medical . . . . médico *(also used for "doctor,"*
                                    "medic")
metaphorical. . . . . metafórico
metaphysical. . . . . metafísico
methodical . . . . metódico
musical. . . . . músico
mystical . . . . místico
mythical . . . . mítico
mythological . . . . mitológico

nautical . . . . náutico
neurological . . . . neurológico
numerical . . . . numérico

optical . . . . óptico

paradoxical . . . . paradójico
pathological . . . . patológico
pedagogical . . . . pedagógico
periodical . . . . periódico *(also used for "newspaper")*
pharmaceutical . . . . farmaceutico *(also used for "pharmacist")*
philosophical . . . . filosófico
physical . . . . físico
physiological . . . . fisiológico
poetical . . . . poético
political . . . . político
practical . . . . **práctico**
   "She is very practical." . . . . . **"Ella es muy práctica".**
prehistorical . . . . prehistórico
psychological . . . . psicológico

reciprocal . . . . recíproco
rhetorical . . . . retórico
rhythmical . . . . rítmico

sabbatical . . . . sabático
satirical . . . . satírico
skeptical . . . . escéptico
sociological . . . . sociológico
sociopolitical . . . . sociopolítico
spherical . . . . esférico
statistical . . . . estadístico
stereotypical . . . . estereotípico
stoical . . . . estoico
strategical . . . . estratégico
symmetrical . . . . simétrico

tactical . . . . táctico
technical . . . . **técnico** *(also used for "technician")*
technological . . . . tecnológico
theological . . . . teológico

theoretical . . . . teórico

topical . . . . tópico

typical . . . . **típico**

    "What a typical response!" . . . **"¡Qué respuesta típica!"**

typographical . . . . tipográfico

tyrannical . . . . tiránico

Una las palabras que están relacionadas o que son sinónimos.

1. típico	pragmático
2. idéntico	importante
3. práctico	usual
4. biográfico	personal
5. diabólico	médico
6. clínico	demoníaco
7. crítico	igual

Escuche y lea el cuento. Responda las siguientes preguntas, usando oraciones completas.

Juan dice, "Alicante es tan bonita que podemos pasar el mes entero (the whole month) aquí". Angélica comprende pero dice, "No, quiero ser práctica, debemos continuar nuestro viaje de una manera lógica". Juan ve que ella es muy lógica ahora y dice, "Angélica, ésto es típico de tí, ¡eres siempre tan práctica!" Ella responde, "¡No seas tan crítico! Tú también quieres ir a la Costa del Sol, ¿verdad?" Juan responde, "Tienes razón (you're right), vamos a la Costa del Sol".

1. ¿ Juan quiere permanecer (to stay) en Alicante o partir?

-ical/-ico

2. ¿De qué manera quiere viajar Angélica?

3. ¿Angélica es siempre práctica?

4. ¿Adónde van ahora?

5. ¿Qué dice Angélica de la Costa del Sol?

Chapter 13

Many English words ending in "–id" correspond to "–ido" in Spanish.

Spanish words ending in "–ido" are usually adjectives. For example,

a <u>splendid</u> plan = *un plan <u>espléndido</u>*

ENGLISH . . . . SPANISH	

All words and phrases in **bold** *are on* **Track 13** *of the accompanying audio.*

acid	ácido
antacid	antiácido
arid	árido
avid	ávido
candid	cándido *(meaning "innocent," "naïve")*
Cupid	Cupido
fervid	férvido
flaccid	flácido
florid	florido
fluid	fluido
frigid	frígido
hybrid	híbrido
insipid	insípido
intrepid	intrépido
invalid	inválido
languid	lánguido

liquid . . . . **líquido**
livid . . . . lívido
lucid . . . . lúcido

morbid . . . . mórbido

pallid . . . . pálido
placid . . . . plácido
putrid . . . . pútrido

rapid . . . . **rápido**
rigid. . . . . **rígido**

solid . . . . sólido
sordid . . . . sórdido
splendid . . . . **espléndido**
      "He has a splendid plan." . . . **"El tiene un plan espléndido"**.
squallid . . . . escuálido
stupid. . . . . **estúpido**

timid . . . . **tímido**
      "Mateo is very timid." . . . . . . **"Mateo es muy tímido"**.
torrid . . . . tórrido

valid . . . . **válido**
vivid . . . . vívido

13A.

Una las palabras que están relacionadas o que son sinónimos.

1. rápido   maravilloso
2. tímido   limón
3. estúpido   veloz
4. ácido   introvertido
5. frígido   seco
6. árido   helado
7. espléndido   idiota

13B.

Escuche y lea el cuento. Responda las siguientes preguntas, usando oraciones completas.

Para ir a la Costa del Sol, Juan y Angélica deciden alquilar (to rent) **otro carro. Angélica dice que es un plan** estúpido**, pero Juan piensa que es un plan** espléndido**. Angélica dice, "Pero yo quiero viajar mas** rápido**… ". Juan dice que prefiere conducir cuando hace calor. Durante el viaje hace un tiempo** (the weather is) **muy** húmedo**; de repente Juan se pone muy** pálido **y le duele el estómago. Angélica no dice nada y va a una farmacia y compra un poco de** antiácido **para Juan. El farmacéutico dice que él debe beber mucho** líquido **y no comer comida** ácida**.**

1. ¿Qué dice Angélica del plan de ir a la Costa del Sol en carro?

2. ¿Qué piensa Juan de su idea?

3. ¿Qué tiempo hace durante el viaje?

4. ¿Qué le compra Angélica a Juan cuando él se siente mal?

5. ¿El farmacéutico dice que debe beber qué? ¿Y qué no debe comer?

Chapter 14

English words ending in "–ism" often correspond to "–ismo" in Spanish.

Spanish words ending in "–ismo" are usually masculine nouns. For example,

optimism = *el optimismo*

ENGLISH....... SPANISH	

All words and phrases in **bold** are on **Track 14** of the accompanying audio.

absenteeism	absentismo
absolutism	absolutismo
activism	activismo
adventurism	aventurismo
alcoholism	**alcoholismo**
altruism	altruismo
Americanism.	americanismo
amorphism	amorfismo
anachronism.	anacronismo
anarchism.	anarquismo
Anglicism	anglicismo
antagonism.	antagonismo
anticapitalism	anticapitalismo
anticommunism	anticomunismo
antifascism	**antifascismo**

    "There was a lot of antifascism.". . . **"Había mucho antifascismo"**.

anti-Semitism.	antisemitismo
antiterrorism	antiterrorismo
astigmatism.	astigmatismo
atheism	ateísmo
athleticism	**atletismo** *(also used for "track-and-field")*
autism	autismo

baptism . . . . bautismo
bipolarism . . . . bipolarismo
botulism . . . . botulismo
Buddhism . . . . budismo

cannibalism . . . . canibalismo
capitalism . . . . **capitalismo**
   "Capitalism comes   **"El capitalismo viene**
      from America." . . . . **de América".**
Catholicism . . . . catolicismo
catechism . . . . catecismo
centralism . . . . centralismo
chauvinism . . . . chovinismo
classicism . . . . clasicismo
colonialism . . . . colonialismo
communism . . . . **comunismo**
conformism . . . . conformismo
conservatism . . . . conservatismo
criticism . . . . criticismo *(more commonly "crítica")*
cubism . . . . cubismo
cynicism . . . . cinismo

Darwinism . . . . darwinismo
deism . . . . deísmo
despotism . . . . despotismo
determinism . . . . determinismo
dogmatism . . . . dogmatismo
dualism . . . . dualismo

egoism . . . . egoísmo *(meaning "selfishness")*
egotism . . . . egotismo
elitism . . . . elitismo
eroticism . . . . erotismo
euphemism . . . . eufemismo
evangelism . . . . evangelismo
evolutionism . . . . evolucionismo

INSTANT Spanish Vocabulary Builder

exorcism. . . . . exorcismo
expressionism . . . . expresionismo
extremism . . . . extremismo

fanaticism. . . . . fanatismo
fascism. . . . . **fascismo**
   "I don't like fascism.". . . . . . . **"No me gusta el fascismo"**.
fatalism . . . . fatalismo
favoritism . . . . favoritismo
federalism. . . . . federalismo
feminism . . . . **feminismo**
feudalism . . . . feudalismo
fundamentalism . . . . fundamentalismo
futurism . . . . futurismo

globalism . . . . globalismo

hedonism . . . . hedonismo
heroism . . . . heroísmo
Hinduism . . . . hinduismo
humanism. . . . . humanismo
humanitarianism . . . . humanitarismo
hypnotism. . . . . hipnotismo

idealism . . . . idealismo
imperialism. . . . . imperialismo
impressionism . . . . **impresionismo**
individualism. . . . . individualismo
Italianism . . . . italianismo

Judaism . . . . judaismo

Latinism . . . . latinismo
lesbianism . . . . lesbianismo
liberalism . . . . liberalismo
localism . . . . localismo

magnetism	magnetismo
Marxism	marxismo
materialism	materialismo
mechanism	**mecanismo**
metabolism	metabolismo
microorganism	microorganismo
minimalism	minimalismo
modernism	modernismo
monotheism	monoteísmo
multiculturalism	multiculturalismo

nationalism	**nacionalismo**

"There is a lot of nationalism." . . . **"Hay mucho nacionalismo".**

naturalism	naturalismo
Nazism	nazismo
negativism	negativismo
neofascism	neofascismo
neologism	neologismo
neo-Nazism	neonazismo
neorealism	neorrealismo
nepotism	nepotismo
nudism	nudismo

objectivism	objetivismo
occultism	ocultismo
opportunism	oportunismo
optimism	**optimismo**

"Optimism always helps." . . . **"El optimismo ayuda siempre".**

organism	**organismo**

paganism	paganismo
parallelism	paralelismo
passivism	pasivismo
patriotism	patriotismo
pessimism	pesimismo
pluralism	pluralismo

polytheism	politeísmo
populism	populismo
positivism	positivismo
postmodernism	posmodernismo
pragmatism	pragmatismo
primitivism	primitivismo
professionalism	**profesionalismo**
protectionism	proteccionismo
Protestantism	protestantismo
provincialism	provincialismo
purism	purismo
Puritanism	puritanismo

racism	**racismo**
radicalism	radicalismo
rationalism	racionalismo
realism	realismo
reformism	reformismo
regionalism	regionalismo
relativism	relativismo
romanticism	romanticismo

sadism	sadismo
satanism	satanismo
sensationalism	sensacionalismo
sensualism	sensualismo
separatism	separatismo
sexism	sexismo
socialism	**socialismo**
spiritualism	espiritualismo
Stalinism	estalinismo
stoicism	estoicismo
structuralism	estructuralismo
surrealism	surrealismo
syllogism	silogismo
symbolism	simbolismo

synchronism . . . . sincronismo

terrorism . . . . **terrorismo**
    "Terrorism is senseless." . . . . . **"El terrorismo no tiene sentido".**
totalitarianism . . . . totalitarismo
tourism. . . . . **turismo**
traditionalism . . . . tradicionalismo
transcendentalism . . . . trascendentalismo
traumatism . . . . traumatismo
truism. . . . . truismo

utilitarianism . . . . utilitarismo

vandalism. . . . . vandalismo
vegetarianism . . . . vegetarianismo
voyeurism. . . . . voyeurismo

Una las palabras que están relacionadas o que son sinónimos.

1. turismo   olímpico
2. comunismo   nación
3. patriotismo   Karl Marx
4. atletismo   comentario
5. terrorismo   positivo
6. optimismo   bomba
7. criticismo   vacaciones

Escuche y lea el cuento. Responda las siguientes preguntas, usando oraciones completas.

Después de su primer día en la Costa del Sol, Juan se siente mejor. Hay mucho <u>turismo</u> en la Costa del Sol, y mucha historia, pero ellos deciden relajarse (decide to relax) **por algunos días en la playa. Angélica compra un libro de historia española y lee sobre el comienzo** (about the beginning) **del <u>fascismo</u> en España durante los años treinta. También lee sobre la influencia del <u>comunismo</u> y del <u>socialismo</u> en España. Ellos hablan sobre el <u>patriotismo</u> español, y Angélica le pregunta a Juan qué piensa sobre** (what he thinks about) **el <u>capitalismo</u>. Juan dice, "Angélica, todo esto es muy interesante pero... ¡tomemos un helado!"**

1. ¿Hay mucho turismo en la Costa del Sol?

2. ¿Cuándo comenzó el fascismo en España?

3. ¿ Angélica lee sobre la influencia de qué en España?

4. ¿Sobre qué hablan?

5. ¿Qué dice Juan al final?

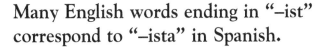

Chapter 15

Many English words ending in "–ist" correspond to "–ista" in Spanish.

Spanish words ending in "–ista" are usually nouns. For example,

an artist = *un/una artista*

ENGLISH . . . . SPANISH	

All words and phrases in **bold** *are on* **Track 15** *of the accompanying audio.*

abolitionist	abolicionista
activist	activista
acupuncturist	acupuncturista
adventurist	aventurista
alchemist	alquemista
altruist	altruista
analyst	analista
anarchist	anarquista
anatomist	anatomista
antagonist	antagonista
anticommunist	anticomunista
antifascist	antifascista
artist	**artista**
"That artist is creative."	**"Ese artista es creativo".**
atheist	ateísta *(more commonly "ateo")*
Baptist	bautista
botanist	botanista
Buddhist	budista
capitalist	**capitalista**
caricaturist	caricaturista

cellist	violoncelista
centralist	centralista
chauvinist	chovinista
columnist	columnista
communist	**comunista**
conformist	conformista
conservationist	conservacionista
contortionist	contorsionista
cubist	cubista
cyclist	ciclista

dentist	**dentista**

"Her son is a dentist." . . . . . . **"Su hijo es un dentista".**

dualist	dualista
duelist	duelista

ecologist	ecologista
economist	economista
egoist	egoísta
egotist	egotista
elitist	elitista
essayist	ensayista
evangelist	evangelista
exhibitionist	exhibicionista
existentialist	existencialista
expansionist	expansionista
expressionist	expresionista
extremist	extremista

fascist	fascista
fatalist	fatalista
federalist	federalista
feminist	feminista
finalist	**finalista**
flutist	flautista
florist	**florista**

formalist . . . . formalista
fundamentalist. . . . . fundamentalista
futurist . . . . futurista

geneticist . . . . geneticista
guitarist . . . . **guitarrista**
    "Carlos Santana is   **"Carlos Santana es**
    a great guitarist." . . . . **un gran guitarrista".**

harpist . . . . arpista
hedonist . . . . hedonista
humanist. . . . . humanista
humorist . . . . humorista
hygienist. . . . . higienista

idealist. . . . . **idealista**
illusionist . . . . ilusionista
imperialist. . . . . imperialista
impressionist . . . . impresionista
individualist . . . . individualista
internist . . . . internista
isolationist . . . . aislacionista

jurist. . . . . jurista

Latinist . . . . latinista
Leninist. . . . . leninista
linguist . . . . lingüista
list . . . . **lista**
    "She has a list of questions." . . . **"Ella tiene una lista de preguntas".**

machinist . . . . maquinista
manicurist. . . . . manicurista
Marxist . . . . marxista
masochist . . . . masoquista
materialist. . . . . materialista

Methodist	metodista
minimalist	**minimalista**
modernist	modernista
monopolist	monopolista
moralist	moralista
motorist	motorista
muralist	muralista
narcissist	narcisista
nationalist	nacionalista
naturalist	naturalista
novelist	novelista
nudist	nudista
nutritionist	**nutricionista**
opportunist	oportunista
optimist	**optimista**
organist	organista
orthodontist	ortodontista
pacifist	pacifista
perfectionist	perfeccionista
pessimist	**pesimista**
pianist	**pianista**

"He wants to be a pianist." . . **"Quisiera ser pianista"**.

pluralist	pluralista
populist	populista
positivist	positivista
pragmatist	pragmatista
prohibitionist	prohibicionista
protagonist	protagonista
protectionist	proteccionista
publicist	publicista
purist	purista
racist	**racista**

rationalist . . . . racionalista
realist. . . . . **realista**
receptionist. . . . . recepcionista
reformist. . . . . reformista
reservist . . . . reservista

sadomasochist . . . . sadomasoquista
satanist. . . . . satanista
satirist . . . . satirista
secessionist. . . . . secesionista
semifinalist . . . . semifinalista
separatist . . . . separatista
sexist . . . . sexista
socialist . . . . socialista
soloist . . . . solista
specialist . . . . especialista
Stalinist . . . . estalinista
stylist . . . . estilista
surrealist. . . . . surrealista
symbolist . . . . simbolista

terrorist . . . . **terrorista**
tourist . . . . **turista**
   "In Spain, I'm a tourist." . . . . **"En España, soy turista".**
traditionalist . . . . tradicionalista

violinist. . . . . violinista
vocalist. . . . . vocalista

15A.

Una las palabras que están relacionadas o que son sinónimos.

1. artista	dinero
2. dentista	pasaporte
3. turista	campeón
4. pesimista	cantante
5. idealista	positivo
6. finalista	diente
7. capitalista	negativo

15B.

Escuche y lea el cuento. Responda las siguientes preguntas, usando oraciones completas.

Destinación: ¡Andalucía! Mientras Juan y Angélica pasean por (walk around) **Andalucía conocen otra pareja** (another couple) **de Bilbao. El muchacho es <u>dentista</u> y la muchacha es <u>artista</u>; los nuevos amigos de Juan y Angélica son <u>turistas</u> "profesionales"; viajan mucho y saben mucho sobre Andalucía. Angélica tiene una <u>lista</u> de preguntas y el <u>dentista</u> puede dar una respuesta a cada** (every) **pregunta. Son muy inteligentes pero son una pareja extraña. La muchacha es <u>optimista</u> mientras que el muchacho es <u>pesimista</u>. Ella es <u>idealista</u> y él es <u>realista</u>. El <u>dentista</u> les dice a Juan y Angélica, "¿Queréis ir a Málaga con nosostros?" Juan responde, "Veremos...".**

1. ¿Qué hace el muchacho que conocen?

2. ¿Los nuevos amigos de Juan y Angélica viajan a menudo (often)?

3. ¿De qué tiene una lista Angélica?

4. ¿Cómo es el dentista?

5. ¿Cómo es la artista?

-ive/-ivo

English words ending in "–ive" often correspond to "–ivo" in Spanish.

Spanish words ending in "–ivo" are usually adjectives. For example,

a <u>competitive</u> boy = *un niño <u>competitivo</u>*

ENGLISH....... SPANISH	

All words and phrases in **bold** *are on* **Track 16** *of the accompanying audio.*

abortive	abortivo
abrasive	abrasivo
abusive	abusivo
accumulative	acumulativo
accusative	acusativo
active	**activo**
"It's not an active volcano." . . .	**"No es un volcán activo".**
addictive	adictivo
additive	aditivo
adhesive	adhesivo
adjective	**adjetivo**
administrative	administrativo
adoptive	adoptivo
affective	afectivo
affirmative	afirmativo
aggressive	**agresivo**
allusive	alusivo
alternative	alternativo
anticorrosive	anticorrosivo
appositive	apositivo
apprehensive	aprensivo
archive	archivo

assertive . . . . asertivo

associative . . . . asociativo

attractive . . . . atractivo

attributive . . . . atributivo

augmentative . . . . aumentativo

authoritive . . . . autoritativo *(more commonly*
"autoritario")

captive . . . . cautivo

causative . . . . causativo

coactive . . . . coactivo

cognitive . . . . cognitivo

cohesive . . . . cohesivo

collaborative . . . . colaborativo

collective . . . . colectivo

combative . . . . combativo

commemorative . . . . conmemorativo

communicative . . . . comunicativo

comparative . . . . comparativo

competitive . . . . **competitivo**
"The kids are   **"Los niños son**
so competitive." . . . . **tan competitivos".**

comprehensive . . . . comprensivo *(meaning "understanding")*

compulsive . . . . compulsivo

conclusive . . . . conclusivo

conductive . . . . conductivo

conflictive . . . . conflictivo

connective . . . . conectivo

consecutive . . . . **consecutivo**

conservative . . . . conservativo *(more commonly*
"conservador")

constructive . . . . constructivo

contemplative . . . . contemplativo

contributive . . . . contributivo

convulsive . . . . convulsivo

cooperative . . . . **cooperativo**

coordinative . . . . coordinativo
corrective . . . . correctivo
corrosive . . . . corrosivo
corruptive . . . . corruptivo
creative . . . . **creativo**
cumulative . . . . acumulativo
curative . . . . curativo
cursive . . . . cursivo

dative . . . . dativo
decisive . . . . decisivo
declarative . . . . declarativo
decorative . . . . decorativo
deductive . . . . deductivo
defensive . . . . defensivo *(only used to describe things)*
definitive . . . . **definitivo**
 "It's a definitive plan." . . . . . . **"Es un plan definitivo".**
degenerative. . . . . degenerativo
deliberative. . . . . deliberativo
demonstrative . . . . demostrativo
denominative . . . . denominativo
depressive . . . . depresivo
derivative . . . . derivativo
descriptive . . . . descriptivo
destructive . . . . destructivo
determinative . . . . determinativo
diffusive . . . . difusivo
digestive. . . . . digestivo
diminutive. . . . . diminutivo
directive . . . . directivo
distinctive . . . . distintivo
distributive . . . . distributivo
divisive. . . . . divisivo

educative . . . . educativo

effective . . . . efectivo *(also used for "cash")*

elective. . . . . electivo

elusive . . . . elusivo

emotive . . . . emotivo *(meaning "emotional")*

erosive. . . . . erosivo

evasive. . . . . evasivo

evocative . . . . evocativo

excessive . . . . **excesivo**

exclusive . . . . exclusivo

executive . . . . **ejecutivo**

exhaustive . . . . exhaustivo

expansive. . . . . expansivo

explicative . . . . explicativo

explorative . . . . explorativo *(more commonly "exploratorio")*

explosive . . . . explosivo

expressive . . . . expresivo

extensive . . . . extensivo

festive . . . . festivo *(also used for "of a holiday")*

figurative . . . . figurativo

formative . . . . formativo

fugitive. . . . . fugitivo

furtive. . . . . furtivo

generative . . . . generativo

hyperactive. . . . . hiperactivo

illuminative . . . . iluminativo

illustrative . . . . ilustrativo

imaginative. . . . . **imaginativo**

   "What an imaginative plan!". . . **"¡Qué plan tan imaginativo!"**

imitative . . . . imitativo

imperative . . . . imperativo

implosive . . . . implosivo

impulsive	impulsivo
inactive	inactivo
incentive	incentivo
incisive	incisivo
inclusive	inclusivo
indicative	indicativo
infinitive	infinitivo
informative	informativo
inoffensive	inofensivo
inquisitive	inquisitivo
instinctive	instintivo
instructive	instructivo
intensive	intensivo
interactive	**interactivo**
interpretative	interpretativo
interrogative	interrogativo
intransitive	intransitivo
introspective	introspectivo
intuitive	intuitivo
inventive	inventivo
legislative	legislativo
lucrative	lucrativo
massive	masivo
motive	motivo
multiplicative	multiplicativo
narrative	narrativo
native	nativo
negative	**negativo**

"Don't be so negative!" . . . . . **"¡No seas tan negativo!"**

nominative	nominativo
objective	**objetivo**
obsessive	obsesivo

offensive	**ofensivo**
olive	olivo *(meaning "olive tree")*
operative	operativo
oppressive	opresivo
partitive	partitivo
passive	pasivo
pejorative	peyorativo
pensive	pensativo
perceptive	perceptivo
permissive	permisivo
persuasive	persuasivo
positive	**positivo**
possessive	**posesivo**
preparative	preparativo
prescriptive	preceptivo
presumptive	presuntivo
preventive	preventivo
primitive	**primitivo**
productive	**productivo**
progressive	progresivo
prohibitive	prohibitivo
prospective	prospectivo
provocative	provocativo
punitive	punitivo
qualitative	cualitativo
quantitative	cuantitativo
radioactive	radiactivo
reactive	reactivo
receptive	receptivo
recessive	recesivo
recreative	recreativo
reflexive	reflexivo
regressive	regresivo

relative. . . . . relativo *(only an adjective)*

repetitive . . . . **repetitivo**

    "It's a repetitive exercise." . . . **"Es un ejercicio repetitivo".**

repulsive. . . . . repulsivo

representative . . . . representativo *(only an adjective)*

repressive. . . . . represivo

reproductive . . . . reproductivo

respective. . . . . respectivo

restorative. . . . . restaurativo

restrictive . . . . restrictivo

retentive . . . . retentivo

retroactive . . . . retroactivo

retrospective . . . . retrospectivo

sedative . . . . sedativo

seductive . . . . seductivo *(more commonly*
                               "seductor(a)")*

selective . . . . **selectivo**

sensitive . . . . sensitivo *(meaning "perceptive")*

speculative . . . . especulativo

subjective . . . . **subjetivo**

subjunctive . . . . subjuntivo

subversive. . . . . subversivo

successive. . . . . sucesivo

suggestive. . . . . sugestivo *(also used for "attractive")*

superlative . . . . superlativo

tentative . . . . tentativo

transitive. . . . . transitivo

unproductive. . . . . improductivo

vegetative. . . . . vegetativo

votive. . . . . votivo

Una las palabras que están relacionadas o que son sinónimos.

1. creativo	pesimista
2. consecutivo	optimista
3. negativo	imaginativo
4. positivo	siguiente
5. competitivo	causa
6. productivo	ganador
7. motivo	eficiente

Escuche y lea el cuento. Responda las siguientes preguntas, usando oraciones completas.

Juan encuentra a Andalucía absolutamente fascinante. Había escuchado (he had heard) **muchas cosas <u>negativas</u> sobre Andalucía, pero él ve una región <u>creativa</u> y <u>productiva</u>. También Angélica tiene una impresión <u>positiva</u> de Andalucía. Antes de partir Juan quiere ir a buscar el pueblo** (the village) **donde nació su abuelo. "Un buen <u>motivo</u> para ir",
dice Angélica. Van a Jerez, un pueblo poco <u>activo</u> pero muy acogedor** (welcoming). **Pasan dos días <u>consecutivos</u> allí.**

1. ¿Qué había escuchado Juan sobre Andalucía?

2. ¿Qué piensa Juan ahora sobre Andalucía?

3. ¿Qué impresión tiene Angélica de Andalucía?

4. ¿Cómo es el pueblo de Jerez?

5. ¿Cuántos días pasan allí?

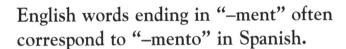

Chapter 17

English words ending in "–ment" often correspond to "–mento" in Spanish.

Spanish words ending in "–mento" are usually masculine nouns. For example,

a monument = *un monumento*

ENGLISH . . . . SPANISH

apartment . . . . **apartamento**
   "What a beautiful apartment." . . . **"¡Qué apartamento tan bonito!"**
argument . . . . argumento *(also used for "plot/story line")*

armament . . . . armamento

cement . . . . **cemento**
compartment . . . . compartimento
complement . . . . complemento
condiment . . . . condimento

department . . . . **departamento** *(also used for "apartment")*
   "I'm looking for   **"Busco el Departamento**
   the Spanish Department." . . . . **de Español".**
detriment . . . . detrimento
document . . . . **documento**

element . . . . **elemento**
excrement . . . . excremento
experiment . . . . experimento

ferment. . . . . fermento *(only a noun)*
filament . . . . filamento
firmament. . . . . firmamento
fragment . . . . **fragmento**

impediment. . . . . impedimento
implement. . . . . implemento
increment . . . . incremento
instrument . . . . **instrumento**

lament . . . . lamento
ligament. . . . . ligamento

microelement . . . . microelemento
moment . . . . **momento**
   "One moment, please." . . . . . **"Un momento, por favor".**
monument . . . . **monumento**

ornament . . . . **ornamento**

parliament . . . . parlamento
pavement . . . . pavimento
pigment . . . . pigmento

rudiment. . . . . rudimento

sacrament. . . . . sacramento
sediment. . . . . sedimento
segment . . . . **segmento**
supplement. . . . . suplemento

temperament. . . . . temperamento
testament . . . . testamento
torment. . . . . tormento

Sometimes English words ending in "–ment" will correspond to "–miento" in Spanish. Following are seventeen (17) of the most commonly used words that follow this pattern:

commandment > mandamiento
comportment > comportamiento
discernment > discernimiento
enchantment > encantamiento
enrichment > enriquecimiento
entertainment > entretenimiento
equipment > equipamiento
establishment > establecimiento
movement > movimiento
presentiment > presentimiento
recruitment > reclutamiento
refinement > refinamiento
regiment > regimiento
requirement > requerimiento
resentment > resentimiento
sentiment > sentimiento
treatment > tratamiento

Una las palabras que están relacionadas o que son sinónimos.

1. instrumento	medicina
2. apartamento	papel
3. momento	renta
4. documento	instante
5. tratamiento	guitarra
6. segmento	héroes
7. monumento	parte

Escuche y lea el cuento. Responda las siguientes preguntas, usando oraciones completas.

En camino hacia el norte (on the way north) **el argumento era si ir a Córdoba o no. El tío de Angélica vive allá y tiene un apartamento para ellos. Él es profesor en el departamento de finanzas en la universidad en Córdoba. El problema es que él siempre tiene algún comentario sobre el comportamiento de ellos. Él es muy formal, y nunca da un halago** (compliment)**. Juan no quiere ir porque piensa que será un tormento. Angélica dice, "Vamos, Juan, hazme este favor** (do me this favor)**, y después vamos adonde tú quieras". Por un momento Juan quiere decir que no, pero al final dice, "Está bien, cariño, vamos a Córdoba".**

1. ¿Cuál es el argumento en camino hacia el norte?

2. ¿Dónde vive el tío de Angélica?

3. ¿Qué hace su tío?

4. ¿Por qué Juan no quiere ir a Córdoba?

5. Al final, ¿deciden ir a Córdoba o no?

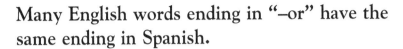

Many English words ending in "–or" have the same ending in Spanish.

Spanish words ending in "–or" are usually masculine nouns. For example,

a motor = *un motor*

ENGLISH . . . . SPANISH

All words and phrases in
bold are on **Track 18** of the
accompanying audio.

accelerator . . . . acelerador

accumulator . . . . acumulador *(also used for "car battery")*

actor . . . . **actor**

    "He's a good actor." . . . . **"Es buen actor".**

adaptor . . . . adaptador

administrator. . . . . administrador

aggressor. . . . . agresor

agitator . . . . agitador

alternator . . . . alternador

ambassador . . . . embajador

animator. . . . . animador *(also used for "presenter")*

anterior . . . . anterior

applicator. . . . . aplicador

ardor . . . . ardor

aspirator . . . . aspirador *(also used for
"vacuum cleaner")*

assessor . . . . asesor *(meaning "consultant")*

auditor. . . . . auditor

author . . . . **autor**

aviator . . . . aviador

benefactor . . . . benefactor

calculator . . . . calculador

calibrator . . . . calibrador

candor . . . . candor *(meaning "innocence")*

cantor . . . . cantor

captivator . . . . cautivador

carburator . . . . carburador

censor . . . . censor

clamor . . . . clamor

co-editor . . . . coeditor

collaborator . . . . colaborador

collector . . . . coleccionador

color . . . . **color**

    "What a nice color." . . . . **"Qué color tan bonito".**

commentator . . . . comentador

communicator . . . . comunicador

competitor . . . . competidor

condor . . . . cóndor

conductor . . . . conductor *(for music, use "director")*

confessor . . . . confesor

connector . . . . conectador

conquistador . . . . conquistador

constructor . . . . constructor

contaminator . . . . contaminador

contributor . . . . contribuidor

cooperator . . . . cooperador

coordinator . . . . coordinador

corrector . . . . corrector

corruptor . . . . corruptor

creator . . . . **creador**

cultivator . . . . cultivador

cursor . . . . cursor

debtor . . . . deudor

decorator . . . . decorador

denominator . . . . denominador

detonator	detonador
detractor	detractor
devastator	devastador
dictator	**dictador**
director	**director**
dishonor	deshonor
distributor	distribuidor
divisor	divisor
doctor	**doctor**
dolor	dolor *(meaning "pain")*
donor	donador
editor	editor
educator	educador
elector	elector
elevator	elevador
emperor	emperador
equator	ecuador
error	**error**
"It's a big error."	**"Es un gran error".**
excavator	excavador
exterior	**exterior**
exterminator	exterminador
extractor	extractor
facilitator	facilitador
factor	factor
favor	**favor**
fervor	fervor
fumigator	fumigador
furor	furor
generator	generador
gladiator	gladiador
governor	gobernador

honor . . . . honor

horror . . . . **horror**

humor . . . . humor *(also used for "mood" and "temper")*

illuminator . . . . iluminador

illustrator . . . . ilustrador

imitator . . . . imitador

impostor . . . . impostor

improvisor . . . . improvisador

incinerator . . . . incinerador

indicator . . . . indicador

inferior . . . . **inferior** *(also used for "lower")*

initiator . . . . iniciador

innovator . . . . **innovador**

inspector . . . . inspector

instigator . . . . instigador

instructor . . . . instructor

interceptor . . . . interceptor

interior . . . . **interior**

interlocutor . . . . interlocutor

interrogator . . . . interrogador

interruptor . . . . interruptor *(also used for "electrical switch")*

inventor . . . . **inventor**

   "Thomas Edison was   **"Thomas Edison fue**
   an inventor." . . . . **un inventor".**

investigator . . . . investigador

laminator . . . . laminador

legislator . . . . legislador

liberator . . . . libertador

liquidator . . . . liquidador

liquor . . . . licor

major . . . . mayor *(meaning "bigger" or "older")*

manipulator	manipulador
matador	matador
mediator	mediador
mentor	mentor
minor	menor *(also used for "smaller" or "younger")*
mitigator	mitigador
moderator	moderador
monitor	monitor
motor	**motor**
multicolor	multicolor
narrator	narrador
navigator	navegador *(more commonly "navegante")*
negotiator	negociador
odor	**olor** *(also used for "scent")*
operator	operador
oppressor	opresor
orator	orador
pastor	pastor
persecutor	perseguidor
possessor	poseedor
posterior	posterior
preceptor	preceptor
precursor	precursor
predator	depredador
predecessor	predecesor
processor	procesador
procreator	procreador
professor	**profesor** *(also used for "teacher")*
projector	proyector
propagator	propagador
protector	**protector**

Chapter 18

radiator	radiador
rancor	rencor
raptor	raptor
reactor	reactor
receptor	receptor
rector	rector
reflector	reflector
refrigerator	refrigerador
regulator	regulador
renovator	renovador
repressor	represor
respirator	respirador
resuscitator	resucitador
rigor	rigor
rotor	rotor
rumor	rumor *(also used for "murmur")*
savior	salvador
sculptor	escultor
sector	sector
selector	selector
semiconductor	semiconductor
senator	**senador**
sensor	sensor
separator	separador
simulator	simulador
spectator	espectador
speculator	especulador
splendor	esplendor
stupor	estupor
successor	sucesor
superior	superior *(also used for "upper")*
supervisor	supervisor
suppressor	supresor
technicolor	tecnicolor

tenor . . . . tenor
terminator . . . . terminador
terror . . . . **terror**
tractor . . . . tractor
traitor . . . . traidor
transgressor . . . . transgresor
transistor . . . . transistor
translator . . . . traductor
tremor . . . . temblor
tricolor . . . . tricolor
tumor . . . . **tumor**
　　"It's a benign tumor." . . . . **"Es un tumor benigno"**.
tutor . . . . tutor *(also used for "guardian")*

ulterior . . . . ulterior

valor . . . . valor
vapor . . . . **vapor**
vector . . . . vector
vendor . . . . vendedor
ventilator . . . . ventilador *(meaning "electric fan")*
violator . . . . violador *(also used for "rapist")*
vibrator . . . . vibrador
vigor . . . . vigor

Una las palabras que están relacionadas o que son sinónimos.

1. motor	gracias
2. color	afuera
3. favor	coche
4. terror	libro
5. autor	patente
6. inventor	horror
7. exterior	verde

Escuche y lea el cuento. Responda las siguientes preguntas, usando oraciones completas.

Apenas llegan a Córdoba, el tío les dice que habrá una fiesta en su casa esa noche. Angélica nota inmediatamente el <u>terror</u> en la cara de Juan. Cuando están sólos, Juan dice, "¡Qué <u>error</u> venir aquí! Hazme un <u>favor</u> y dime que no tengo que ir (I don't have to go) **a esa fiesta". Angélica ni siquiera responde** (doesn't even respond) **y Juan comprende que debe ir. La "fiesta" es muy difícil para Juan. Cada dos minutos, el tío dice, "Aquel hombre es <u>doctor</u>, aquel allá es <u>profesor</u>, el otro es <u>inventor</u>". Por un momentito Juan se interesa** (he's interested) **cuando el tío dice, "El <u>senador</u> va a venir con un <u>actor</u> muy famoso". Pero el <u>actor</u> no es famoso y el <u>senador</u> es muy, muy viejo.**

1. ¿Qué nota Angélica en la cara de Juan?

2. ¿Qué dice Juan sobre la decisión de ir a Córdoba?

3. ¿Qué dice Juan sobre la fiesta?

4. ¿El actor es famoso?

5. ¿El senador es joven?

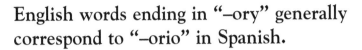

Chapter 19

English words ending in "–ory" generally correspond to "–orio" in Spanish.

Spanish words ending in "–orio" are usually adjectives or masculine nouns. For example,

contradictory (adj.) = *contradictorio*
laboratory (n.) = *el laboratorio*

ENGLISH. . . . . . . SPANISH

All words and phrases in **bold** *are on* **Track 19** *of the accompanying audio.*

accessory . . . . **accesorio**
   "She's buying an accessory." . . . **"Ella compra un accesorio".**
accusatory . . . . acusatorio
ambulatory . . . . ambulatorio
anti-inflammatory . . . . antiinflammatorio

circulatory . . . . circulatorio
combinatory . . . . combinatorio
compensatory . . . . compensatorio
conservatory . . . . conservatorio
contradictory . . . . **contradictorio**
   "It's a contradictory response." . . . **"Es una respuesta contradictoria".**
crematory . . . . crematorio

defamatory . . . . difamatorio
directory . . . . directorio
discriminatory . . . . discriminatorio
dormitory . . . . dormitorio

illusory . . . . ilusorio

inflammatory . . . . inflamatorio
introductory . . . . introductorio

laboratory . . . . **laboratorio**
lavatory . . . . lavatorio

migratory . . . . migratorio

obligatory . . . . **obligatorio**
observatory . . . . observatorio
oratory . . . . oratorio

peremptory . . . . perentorio
predatory . . . . depredatorio
preparatory . . . . preparatorio
promissory . . . . promisorio
promontory . . . . promontorio
provisory . . . . provisorio *(more commonly
"provisional")*

purgatory . . . . **purgatorio**
  "Dante wrote about   **"Dante escribió del
    purgatory."** . . . . **purgatorio".**

reformatory . . . . reformatorio
repertory . . . . repertorio
repository . . . . repositorio
respiratory . . . . respiratorio

satisfactory . . . . satisfactorio
suppository . . . . supositorio

territory . . . . **territorio**
transitory . . . . transitorio

unsatisfactory . . . . insatisfactorio

Una las palabras que están relacionadas o que son sinónimos.

1. accesorio   zona
2. territorio   aretes
3. dormitorio   telescopio
4. laboratorio   insulto
5. observatorio   prólogo
6. derogatorio   experimento
7. introductorio   cama

Escuche y lea el cuento. Responda las siguientes preguntas, usando oraciones completas.

Juan está muy contento cuando finalmente parten de Córdoba hacia Sevilla. Dice, "Hubiera preferido (I'd have preferred) **un hostal".
Angélica admite que fue un <u>territorio</u> extraño. Juan dice, "Pero, ¿qué dices? ¡Fue peor que el <u>purgatorio</u>!" Angélica responde, "No tenías que** (you didn't have to) **venir, no era <u>obligatorio</u>".** Juan se ríe de ese comentario <u>contradictorio</u> pero no responde. Juan dice, "Entonces me **debes** (you owe me) **un favor, ¿verdad?" Angélica dice, "Veremos...".**

1. ¿Adónde van después de Córdoba?

2. ¿Qué hubiera preferido Juan?

3. Juan dice que la fiesta fue peor que ¿qué?

4. ¿Es verdad que su presencia (his presence) no era obligatoria?

5. ¿Responde Juan al último comentario contradictorio de Angélica?

Chapter 20

English words ending in "–ous" generally correspond to "–oso" in Spanish.

Spanish words ending in "–oso" are usually adjectives. For example,

a <u>generous</u> gift = un regalo <u>generoso</u>

ENGLISH . . . . SPANISH

All words and phrases in **bold** *are on* **Track 20** *of the accompanying audio.*

advantageous . . . . ventajoso
ambitious . . . . **ambicioso**
amorous . . . . amoroso
anxious . . . . ansioso

calamitous . . . . calamitoso
callous . . . . calloso
cancerous . . . . canceroso
capricious . . . . caprichoso
cavernous . . . . cavernoso
ceremonious . . . . ceremonioso
clamorous . . . . clamoroso
contagious . . . . contagioso
copious . . . . copioso
curious . . . . **curioso**

decorous . . . . decoroso
delicious . . . . **delicioso**
　　"The food is delicious." . . . . . **"La comida es deliciosa".**
desirous . . . . deseoso
disadvantageous . . . . desventajoso
disastrous . . . . **desastroso**

dubious . . . . dudoso

envious . . . . envidioso

fabulous . . . . fabuloso
famous . . . . famoso
fastidious . . . . fastidioso *(meaning "annoying")*
fibrous . . . . fibroso
furious . . . . **furioso**

gaseous . . . . gaseoso
gelatinous . . . . gelatinoso
generous . . . . **generoso**
    "She is very generous." . . . . . **"Ella es muy generosa".**
glamorous . . . . glamoroso
glorious . . . . glorioso
gracious . . . . gracioso *(meaning "funny")*

harmonious . . . . armonioso

ignominious . . . . ignominioso
impetuous . . . . impetuoso
incestuous . . . . incestuoso
indecorous . . . . indecoroso
industrious . . . . industrioso
ingenious . . . . ingenioso
insidious . . . . insidioso

jealous . . . . celoso
joyous . . . . jubiloso
judicious . . . . juicioso

laborious . . . . laborioso
litigious . . . . litigioso
luminous . . . . luminoso
luxurious . . . . lujoso

malicious	malicioso
marvelous	maravilloso
melodious	melodioso
meticulous	meticuloso
miraculous	milagroso
monstrous	monstruoso
mucous	mucoso
mysterious	**misterioso**

nebulous	nebuloso
nervous	**nervioso**
"Are you nervous?"	**"¿Estás nervioso?"**
numerous	numeroso

obsequious	obsequioso
odious	odioso
onerous	oneroso
ostentatious	ostentoso

perilous	peligroso
pernicious	pernicioso
pious	piadoso
pompous	pomposo
populous	populoso
porous	poroso
portentous	portentoso
precious	**precioso**
prestigious	**prestigioso**
presumptuous	presuntuoso
pretentious	pretencioso
prodigious	prodigioso

rancorous	rencoroso
religious	**religioso**
rigorous	riguroso
ruinous	ruinoso

scabrous	escabroso
scandalous	**escandaloso**
scrupulous	escrupuloso
semiprecious	semiprecioso
sinuous	sinuoso
spacious	**espacioso**
studious	estudioso
sumptuous	suntuoso
superstitious	supersticioso
suspicious	sospechoso
tedious	tedioso
tempestuous	tempestuoso
tortuous	**tortuoso**

"The trip was tortuous." . . . . . **"El viaje fue tortuoso".**

tumultuous	tumultuoso
vaporous	vaporoso
vicious	vicioso *(meaning "depraved,"* *or "addicted")*
victorious	victorioso
vigorous	vigoroso
virtuous	**virtuoso**
viscous	viscoso
voluminous	voluminoso
voluptuous	voluptuoso

INSTANT Spanish Vocabulary Builder

20A.

Una las palabras que están relacionadas o que son sinónimos.

1. curioso	enojado
2. famoso	amplio
3. delicioso	suspenso
4. misterioso	sabroso
5. furioso	inquisitivo
6. precioso	diamante
7. espacioso	celebridad

20B.

Escuche y lea el cuento. Responda las siguientes preguntas, usando oraciones completas.

Después de la visita <u>desastrosa</u> a Córdoba, los dos viajeros están listos para un fin de semana <u>ambicioso</u> en Sevilla. Angélica sabe que este lugar (this place) **es <u>famoso</u> por los churros <u>deliciosos</u>, pero no sabe mucho más de la ciudad. Juan también está muy <u>curioso</u> por conocer a Sevilla. Su amigo le dijo** (told him) **que hay un aire <u>misterioso</u> allí. En la Universidad de Sevilla hay un programa <u>famoso</u> de lenguas extranjeras. Angélica dice, "Cualquiera que estudie** (whoever studies) **en el extranjero debe ser <u>ambicioso</u>". Están en un hotel muy <u>espacioso</u>, y se encuentran muy bien allí. Antes de partir para Toledo, Angélica dice, "Me gusta mucho Sevilla, pero no es un lugar <u>misterioso</u>, ¡tal vez tu amigo es un tipo <u>nervioso</u>!"**

1. ¿Qué tipo de fin de semana quieren pasar en Sevilla?

2. ¿Por qué es famosa Sevilla?

3. ¿Qué dijo el amigo de Juan sobre esta ciudad?

4. ¿Cuál es el programa famoso en la Universidad de Sevilla?

5. ¿Cómo es su hotel?

Chapter 21

English words ending in "–sion" generally correspond to "–sión" in Spanish.

Spanish words ending in "–sión" are usually feminine nouns. For example,

an explosion = *una explosión*

ENGLISH. . . . . . . SPANISH

All words and phrases in **bold** are on **Track 21** of the accompanying audio.

abrasion. . . . . abrasión
adhesion . . . . adhesión
admission. . . . . admisión
aggression . . . . agresión
allusion . . . . alusión
apprehension . . . . aprehensión
ascension . . . . ascensión
aversion . . . . aversión

circumcision . . . . circuncisión
cohesion. . . . . cohesión
collision . . . . **colisión**
   "There was a collision.". . . . . **"Hubo una colisión".**
collusion. . . . . colusión
commission. . . . . comisión
compassion . . . . compasión
comprehension . . . . **comprensión**
compression . . . . compresión
compulsion . . . . compulsión
concession . . . . concesión
conclusion. . . . . **conclusión**
confession . . . . confesión

confusion . . . . **confusión**

contusion . . . . contusión

conversion . . . . conversión

convulsion . . . . convulsión

corrosion . . . . corrosión

decision . . . . **decisión**

decompression . . . . descompresión

depression . . . . depresión

diffusion . . . . difusión

digression . . . . digresión

dimension . . . . **dimensión**

discussion . . . . discusión *(meaning "argument")*

disillusion . . . . desilusión *(also used for*
                                                    "disappointment")

dispersion . . . . dispersión

dissension . . . . disensión

dissuasion . . . . disuasión

diversion . . . . diversión

division . . . . **división**

effusion . . . . efusión

emission . . . . emisión

emulsion . . . . emulsión

erosion . . . . erosión

evasion . . . . evasión *(also used for "escape")*

exclusion . . . . exclusión

excursion . . . . excursión

expansion . . . . expansión

explosion . . . . **explosión**

expression . . . . **expresión**

  "Another idiomatic   **"¡Otra expresión**
    expression!" . . . . **idiomática!"**

expulsion . . . . expulsión

extension . . . . extensión

extroversion . . . . extroversión

fission . . . . fisión

fusion. . . . . fusión *(also used for "merger")*

hypertension . . . . hipertensión

illusion . . . . ilusión
immersion. . . . . inmersión
implosion . . . . implosión
imprecision. . . . . imprecisión
impression . . . . **impresión** *(also used for "printing")*
incision . . . . incisión
inclusion. . . . . inclusión
incomprehension . . . . incomprensión
indecision. . . . . indecisión
infusion . . . . infusión
intercession. . . . . intercesión
intermission. . . . . intermisión *(for shows/theater, use "entreacto")*

introversion. . . . . introversión
intrusion . . . . intrusión
invasion . . . . invasión
inversion. . . . . inversión

lesion. . . . . lesión

mansion . . . . mansión
mission. . . . . **misión**

obsession . . . . obsesión
occasion. . . . . ocasión *(also used for "opportunity")*
occlusion . . . . oclusión
omission. . . . . omisión
oppression . . . . opresión

passion . . . . **pasión**
   "I have a passion for   **"Siento pasión por**
     Spanish." . . . . **el español".**
pension . . . . pensión *(also used for "small hotel")*
percussion . . . . percusión
persuasion . . . . persuasión
perversion . . . . perversión
possession . . . . posesión
precision. . . . . **precisión**
pretension. . . . . pretensión
prevision . . . . previsión
procession . . . . procesión
profession. . . . . **profesión**
profusion . . . . profusión
progression. . . . . progresión
propulsion . . . . propulsión
provision . . . . provisión

recession . . . . recesión
reclusion. . . . . reclusión
regression. . . . . regresión
remission . . . . remisión
repercussion . . . . repercusión
reprehension. . . . . reprensión
repression. . . . . represión
repulsion . . . . repulsión
reversion . . . . reversión
revision . . . . revisión
revulsion. . . . . revulsión *(only used in a medical*
                                      context)

secession . . . . secesión
session . . . . **sesión**
subdivision . . . . subdivisión
submersion . . . . inmersión
submission . . . . sumisión

subversion . . . . subversión
succession . . . . sucesión
supervision . . . . supervisión
suppression. . . . . supresión
suspension . . . . suspensión

television . . . . **televisión**
   "Let's watch television." . . . . . **"Miremos la televisión"**.
tension . . . . **tensión**
transfusion . . . . transfusión
transgression. . . . . transgresión
transmission . . . . transmisión

version . . . . versión
vision . . . . **visión**

Una las palabras que están relacionadas o que son sinónimos.

1. confusión	caos
2. misión	bomba
3. televisión	antena
4. explosión	objetivo
5. pasión	ojo
6. precisión	exactitud
7. visión	amor

Escuche y lea el cuento. Responda las siguientes preguntas, usando oraciones completas.

Apenas llegan a Toledo, Angélica declara, "Tenemos una misión clara aquí en Toledo. Tú sabes que la cerámica es una pasión mía, ¿verdad? Tengo que encontrar (I must find) un plato de cerámica nuevo para mi colección". Juan dice, "Está bien, pero ¿tal vez lo podemos encontrar en La Coruña?" Angélica insiste, "¡NO! ¡Mi decisión es final! Quiero un plato de Toledo". Juan tiene la impresión de que Angélica no está bromeando (isn't kidding around), y él se dedica a la "misión del plato". Después de un almuerzo fabuloso en la plaza ellos comienzan la caza (the hunt). Había un poco de confusión con todas las callejuelas y callejones, pero al final hay una conclusión feliz— Angélica encuentra su plato.

1. ¿Cuál es la misión de Angélica?

2. ¿Por qué quiere eso?

3. ¿Qué dice Angélica de su decisión?

4. ¿Qué impresión tiene Juan de Angélica?

5. ¿Por qué había un poco de confusión?

Chapter 22

English words ending in "–sis" often have the same ending in Spanish.

Spanish words ending in "–sis" are usually nouns. For example,

an analysis = *un análisis*

ENGLISH . . . . SPANISH

All words and phrases in **bold** *are on* **Track 22** *of the accompanying audio.*

analysis . . . . **análisis**
antithesis . . . . antítesis

biogenesis . . . . biogénesis

catalysis . . . . catálisis
catharsis . . . . catarsis
chassis . . . . chasís
cirrhosis . . . . cirrosis
crisis . . . . **crisis**

diagnosis . . . . diagnosis
dialysis . . . . **diálisis**

electrolysis . . . . electrólisis
emphasis . . . . **énfasis**
  "You need more emphasis." . . . **"Necesitas más énfasis".**

fibrosis . . . . fibrosis

genesis . . . . **génesis**

halitosis . . . . halitosis
hydrolysis . . . . hidrólisis
hypnosis . . . . **hipnosis**
hypothesis . . . . **hipótesis**
    "What is your hypothesis?" . . . **"¿Cúal es tu hipótesis?"**

macroanalysis . . . . macroanálisis
metamorphosis . . . . **metamorfosis**
metastasis . . . . metástasis
microanalysis . . . . microanálisis
mononucleosis . . . . mononucleosis

narcosis . . . . narcosis
nemesis . . . . némesis
neurosis . . . . neurosis

oasis . . . . oasis
osmosis . . . . ósmosis
osteoporosis . . . . osteoporosis

paralysis . . . . parálisis
parenthesis . . . . paréntesis
photogenesis . . . . fotogénesis
photosynthesis . . . . fotosíntesis
prognosis . . . . prognosis
prosthesis . . . . prótesis
psoriasis . . . . psoriasis
psychoanalysis . . . . psicoanálisis
psychosis . . . . psicosis

sclerosis . . . . esclerosis
scoliosis . . . . escoliosis
self-analysis . . . . autoanálisis
synopsis . . . . sinopsis
synthesis . . . . síntesis

INSTANT Spanish Vocabulary Builder

thesis . . . . **tesis**
    "Did he write his thesis?" . . . . **"¿Él escribió la tesis?"**
tuberculosis . . . . tuberculosis

Una las palabras que están relacionadas o que son sinónimos.

1. crisis	soñar
2. tuberculosis	enfermedad
3. énfasis	cambio
4. parálisis	dificultad
5. hipnosis	inmovilidad
6. metamorfosis	acento
7. análisis	estudio

Escuche y lea el cuento. Responda las siguientes preguntas, usando oraciones completas.

Destinación: ¡Madrid! Juan y Angélica ya conocen a (already know) **Madrid bastante bien. Entonces no ponen mucho <u>énfasis</u> en el giro turístico. Van a buscar, en cambio, a un primo de Juan que estudia en Madrid. Se llama Carlos y estudia economía. Escribe su <u>tesis</u> sobre la <u>crisis</u> financiera del tercer mundo** (of the Third World)**. Juan y Angélica cenan en casa de Carlos y escuchan mientras Carlos habla largo y tendido sobre su <u>análisis</u> de la <u>crisis</u>. Carlos dice, "Desafortunadamente, no tengo una <u>hipótesis</u> propia sobre como mejorar** (to improve) **la <u>crisis</u>, y sin esta <u>hipótesis</u> ¡no puedo hacer mi <u>tesis</u>!" Carlos pregunta a Juan, "¿Puedes ayudarme?" Juan responde, "Veremos…".**

1. ¿Por qué no ponen mucho énfasis en el giro turístico en Madrid?

2. ¿Sobre qué escribe la tesis Carlos?

3. ¿Carlos habla mucho sobre su análisis?

4. ¿Tiene Carlos una buena hipótesis para su tesis?

5. ¿Qué pregunta Carlos a Juan?

-tion/-ción

English words that end in "–tion" often correspond to "–ción" in Spanish.

Spanish words ending in "–ción" are usually feminine nouns. For example,

an operation = *una operación*

ENGLISH. . . . . . . SPANISH

All words and phrases in **bold** *are on* **Track 23** *of the accompanying audio.*

abbreviation . . . . abreviación *(meaning "a shortening")*

abdication . . . . abdicación

aberration . . . . aberración

abolition. . . . . abolición

abomination . . . . abominación

absolution. . . . . absolución

absorption . . . . absorción

abstention. . . . . abstención

abstraction . . . . abstracción

acceleration . . . . aceleración

acclamation . . . . aclamación

accommodation. . . . . acomodación *(more commonly "alojamiento," for lodging)*

accreditation. . . . . acreditación

acculturation . . . . aculturación

accumulation . . . . acumulación

accusation . . . . acusación

acquisition . . . . adquisición

action. . . . . **acción** *(also used for "stock share")*

   "There's not a lot of action." . . . **"No hay mucha acción".**

activation . . . . activación

actualization . . . . actualización
adaptation . . . . adaptación
addiction . . . . adicción
addition . . . . adición
administration . . . . administración
admiration . . . . admiración
admonition . . . . admonición
adoption . . . . adopción
adoration . . . . adoración
adulation . . . . adulación
adulteration . . . . adulteración
affiliation . . . . afiliación
affirmation . . . . afirmación
affliction . . . . aflicción
agitation . . . . agitación
alienation . . . . alienación
alliteration . . . . aliteración
alteration . . . . alteración
ambition . . . . **ambición**
   "They have ambition." . . . . . . **"Tienen ambición".**
Americanization . . . . americanización
amputation . . . . amputación
animation . . . . animación
annotation . . . . anotación
anticipation . . . . anticipación
apparition . . . . aparición
application . . . . aplicación *(for "application form,"*
                                            use "solicitud")
appreciation . . . . apreciación
approbation . . . . aprobación
approximation . . . . aproximación
aspiration . . . . aspiración
assimilation . . . . asimilación
association . . . . asociación
attention . . . . **atención** *(also used for*
                                      "attention please!")

attenuation . . . . atenuación

attraction . . . . atracción

attribution . . . . atribución

audition . . . . audición

authentication . . . . autenticación

authorization . . . . autorización

automation . . . . automatización

aviation . . . . aviación *(also used for "air force")*

benediction . . . . bendición

cancellation . . . . cancelación

capitalization . . . . capitalización

celebration . . . . **celebración**

    "It's a big celebration." . . . . . **"Es una gran celebración".**

centralization . . . . centralización

certification . . . . certificación

circulation . . . . circulación

citation . . . . citación

civilization . . . . civilización

classification . . . . clasificación

coaction . . . . coacción

coalition . . . . coalición

codification . . . . codificación

cognition . . . . cognición

cohabitation . . . . cohabitación

collaboration . . . . colaboración

collection . . . . colección

colonization . . . . colonización

coloration . . . . coloración

combination . . . . combinación

commemoration . . . . conmemoración

commiseration . . . . conmiseración

commotion . . . . conmoción

communication . . . . comunicación

compensation . . . . compensación

competition . . . . competición
compilation . . . . compilación
complication . . . . complicación
composition . . . . composición
concentration . . . . concentración
conception . . . . concepción
condensation . . . . condensación
condition . . . . **condición**
conduction . . . . conducción *(also used for "the act*
of guiding")
confection . . . . confección *(meaning "the making of")*
confederation . . . . confederación
confirmation . . . . confirmación
confiscation . . . . confiscación
conformation . . . . conformación
confrontation . . . . confrontación
congregation . . . . congregación
conjugation . . . . conjugación
conjunction . . . . conjunción
connotation . . . . connotación
conservation . . . . conservación
consideration . . . . consideración
consolation . . . . consolación
consolidation . . . . consolidación
constellation . . . . constelación
consternation . . . . consternación
constipation . . . . constipación *(meaning "head*
congestion")
constitution . . . . constitución
constriction . . . . constricción
construction . . . . construcción
consummation . . . . consumación
contamination . . . . contaminación *(also used for "pollution")*
contemplation . . . . contemplación
contention . . . . contención *(meaning "retention")*
continuation . . . . continuación

contraction . . . . contracción
contradiction . . . . contradicción
contribution . . . . contribución
contrition . . . . contrición
convention . . . . convención
conversation . . . . **conversación**
conviction . . . . convicción
cooperation . . . . cooperación
coordination . . . . **coordinación**
coproduction . . . . coproducción
coronation . . . . coronación
corporation . . . . corporación
correction . . . . corrección
correlation . . . . correlación
corruption . . . . corrupción
creation . . . . creación
cremation . . . . cremación
crystallization . . . . cristalización
culmination . . . . culminación
cumulation . . . . acumulación

decapitation . . . . decapitación
deceleration . . . . desaceleración
decentralization . . . . descentralización
deception . . . . decepción *(meaning "disappointment")*
declamation . . . . declamación
declaration . . . . declaración
declination . . . . declinación
decomposition . . . . descomposición
decoration . . . . decoración
dedication . . . . dedicación
deduction . . . . deducción
defamation . . . . difamación
definition . . . . **definición**
deflation . . . . deflación *(only used in an economic context)*

deforestation . . . . desforestación
deformation . . . . deformación
degeneration . . . . degeneración
degradation . . . . degradación
dehumanization . . . . deshumanización
dehydration . . . . deshidratación
delegation . . . . delegación
deliberation . . . . deliberación
delimitation. . . . . delimitación
demarcation . . . . demarcación
demolition . . . . demolición
demonstration . . . . demostración
denomination . . . . denominación
deportation. . . . . deportación
depravation . . . . depravación
depreciation . . . . depreciación
description . . . . descripción
desertion . . . . deserción
desolation. . . . . desolación
desperation . . . . desesperación
destabilization . . . . desestabilización
destination . . . . destinación
destitution. . . . . destitución *(meaning "dismissal")*
destruction . . . . **destrucción**
detention . . . . detención
determination . . . . determinación
devastation. . . . . devastación
deviation . . . . desviación
devotion. . . . . devoción
diction . . . . dicción
differentiation . . . . diferenciación
digestion . . . . digestión
direction. . . . . **dirección** *(also used for
"street address")*
discretion . . . . discreción
discrimination . . . . discriminación

disfunction . . . . disfunción
disintegration . . . . desintegración
disorganization . . . . desorganización
disorientation . . . . desorientación
disposition . . . . disposición
disproportion . . . . desproporción
disqualification . . . . descalificación
dissection . . . . disección
dissertation . . . . disertación
distillation . . . . destilación
distinction . . . . distinción
distraction . . . . distracción
distribution . . . . distribución
diversification . . . . diversificación
documentation . . . . documentación
domination . . . . dominación
donation . . . . donación
dramatization . . . . dramatización
duplication . . . . duplicación
duration . . . . duración

edition . . . . **edición**
    "It's a new edition." . . . . **"Es una nueva edición".**
education . . . . educación *(also used for "manners")*
ejection . . . . eyección *(more commonly "expulsión")*
elaboration . . . . elaboración
election . . . . elección
electrocution . . . . electrocución
elevation . . . . elevación
elimination . . . . eliminación
elocution . . . . elocución
emancipation . . . . emancipación
embarcation . . . . embarcación *(meaning "boat")*
emigration . . . . emigración
emotion . . . . **emoción**
emulation . . . . emulación

enunciation	enunciación
equation	ecuación
erection	erección
erudition	erudición
eruption	erupción
evaluation	evaluación
evaporation	evaporación
evolution	evolución
exaggeration	**exageración**
examination	examinación *(more commonly "examen")*
exasperation	exasperación
excavation	excavación
exception	excepción
exclamation	exclamación
excretion	excreción
execution	ejecución
exhibition	exhibición
exhortation	exhortación
expedition	expedición
exploration	exploración
exportation	exportación
exposition	exposición
extinction	extinción
extraction	extracción
extradition	extradición
exultation	exultación
fabrication	fabricación *(meaning "manufacturing")*
falsification	falsificación
federation	federación
fermentation	fermentación
fertilization	fertilización
fiction	ficción
filtration	filtración
finalization	finalización
fixation	fijación

INSTANT Spanish Vocabulary Builder

fluctuation. . . . . fluctuación

formation . . . . formación *(also used for "training")*

formulation . . . . formulación

fossilization. . . . . fosilización

foundation . . . . **fundación**

fraction . . . . fracción

fragmentation . . . . fragmentación

friction . . . . fricción

fruition . . . . fruición

frustration . . . . frustración

fumigation . . . . fumigación

function . . . . función

generalization. . . . . generalización

generation . . . . **generación**

   "Every generation changes.". . . **"Cada generación cambia"**.

germination . . . . germinación

gestation . . . . gestación

globalization. . . . . globalización

glorification . . . . glorificación

graduation . . . . graduación

gratification . . . . gratificación *(also used for "tip")*

gravitation . . . . gravitación

habitation. . . . . habitación *(meaning "bedroom")*

hallucination . . . . alucinación

humiliation . . . . humillación

identification . . . . identificación

ignition. . . . . ignición

illumination . . . . iluminación

illustration. . . . . ilustración

imagination . . . . imaginación

imitation . . . . **imitación**

    "It's a horrible imitation!" . . . . **"¡Es una mala imitación!"**

immigration . . . . inmigración

imperfection . . . . imperfección

implication . . . . implicación

importation . . . . importación

improvisation . . . . improvisación

inaction . . . . inacción

inauguration . . . . inauguración

incarnation . . . . encarnación

incineration . . . . incineración

inclination . . . . inclinación

incrimination . . . . incriminación

incubation . . . . incubación

indignation . . . . indignación

indiscretion . . . . indiscreción

induction . . . . inducción

infatuation . . . . infatuación *(meaning "vanity")*

infection . . . . infección

infiltration . . . . infiltración

inflamation . . . . inflamación

inflation . . . . inflación

information . . . . **información**

inhibition . . . . inhibición

initiation . . . . iniciación

injection . . . . inyección

innovation . . . . innovación

inquisition . . . . inquisición

inscription . . . . inscripción *(also used for "enrollment,"*
                                                  "registration")

insemination . . . . inseminación

insertion . . . . inserción

inspection . . . . inspección

inspiration . . . . inspiración

installation . . . . instalación

institution . . . . institución

instruction . . . . instrucción
insurrection . . . . insurrección
integration . . . . integración
intensification . . . . intensificación
intention . . . . **intención**
interaction . . . . interacción
interception . . . . interceptación
interpretation . . . . interpretación
interrogation . . . . interrogación
interruption . . . . interrupción
intersection . . . . intersección
intervention . . . . intervención *(also used for "surgery")*
intimidation . . . . intimidación
intonation . . . . entonación
intoxication . . . . intoxicación *(meaning "poisoning")*
introduction . . . . introducción
introspection . . . . introspección
intuition . . . . intuición
inundation . . . . inundación
invention . . . . **invención**
investigation . . . . investigación
invitation . . . . invitación
irrigation . . . . irrigación
irritation . . . . irritación *(also used for "rash")*

justification . . . . justificación
juxtaposition . . . . yuxtaposición

lamination . . . . laminación
legalization . . . . legalización
legislation . . . . legislación
levitation . . . . levitación
liberation . . . . liberación
limitation . . . . limitación
liposuction . . . . liposucción
liquidation . . . . liquidación

litigation. . . . . litigación
location . . . . localización
locomotion . . . . locomoción
lotion . . . . **loción**
    "We don't have any more lotion." . . . **"No tenemos más loción"**.
lubrication . . . . lubricación

malformation. . . . . malformación
malnutrition. . . . . malnutrición
manifestation . . . . manifestación *(also used for*
                                      "public demonstration")
manipulation. . . . . manipulación
masturbation . . . . masturbación
maturation . . . . maduración
medication . . . . medicación
meditation . . . . meditación
memorization . . . . memorización
menstruation . . . . menstruación
mention . . . . mención
migration . . . . migración
mitigation. . . . . mitigación
moderation. . . . . moderación
modification . . . . modificación
modulation . . . . modulación
monopolization . . . . monopolización
motion . . . . moción *(meaning "proposal")*
motivation. . . . . motivación
multiplication . . . . multiplicación
mutation. . . . . mutación

narration . . . . narración
nation . . . . **nación**
navigation . . . . navegación
negation. . . . . negación
negotiation . . . . negociación
nomination . . . . nominación

INSTANT Spanish Vocabulary Builder

notation . . . . notación
notion . . . . noción
nutrition . . . . nutrición

objection . . . . objeción
obligation. . . . . obligación
observation. . . . . observación
obstruction . . . . obstrucción
occupation . . . . ocupación
operation . . . . **operación**
    "She needs an operation." . . . **"Ella necesita una operación"**.
opposition . . . . oposición
option . . . . opción
oration . . . . oración
organization . . . . organización
orientation . . . . orientación
ovulation . . . . ovulación
oxidation . . . . oxidación

pagination . . . . paginación
palpitation . . . . palpitación
participation . . . . participación
partition . . . . partición
penetration . . . . penetración
perception . . . . percepción
perfection . . . . perfección
perforation . . . . perforación
perpetuation . . . . perpetuación
persecution . . . . persecución
personalization . . . . personalización
personification . . . . personificación
petition. . . . . petición
pollution . . . . polución
population . . . . **población**
portion . . . . porción

position . . . . **posición** *(for employment, use "puesto")*

"What is his/her position?" . . . **"¿Cúal es su posición?"**

postproduction . . . . posproducción

postulation . . . . postulación

potion . . . . poción

precaution . . . . precaución

precipitation . . . . precipitación

precondition . . . . precondición

predestination . . . . predestinación

prediction . . . . predicción

predilection . . . . predilección

predisposition . . . . predisposición

premeditation . . . . premeditación

premonition . . . . premonición

preoccupation . . . . **preocupación**

preparation . . . . preparación

preposition . . . . preposición

prescription . . . . prescripción

presentation . . . . presentación

preservation . . . . preservación

presumption . . . . presunción

prevention . . . . prevención

privation . . . . privación

privatization . . . . privatización

proclamation . . . . proclamación

procreation . . . . procreación

production . . . . producción

prohibition . . . . prohibición

projection . . . . proyección

proliferation . . . . proliferación

promotion . . . . promoción

pronunciation . . . . pronunciación

proportion . . . . proporción

proposition . . . . proposición

prostitution . . . . prostitución

protection	protección
provocation	provocación
publication	publicación
punctuation	puntuación
purification	purificación
qualification	cualificación
quantification	cuantificación
radiation	radiación
ramification	ramificación
ration	ración
reaction	**reacción**
reactivation	reactivación
realization	realización *(meaning "completion")*
reception	recepción
recommendation	recomendación
recollection	recolección *(meaning "gathering")*
reconciliation	reconciliación
recreation	recreación
recrimination	recriminación
recuperation	recuperación
reduction	reducción
reelection	reelección
reevaluation	reevaluación
refraction	refracción
refrigeration	refrigeración
regulation	regulación
rehabilitation	rehabilitación
reincarnation	reencarnación
relation	relación
relaxation	relajación
renovation	renovación
reorganization	reorganización
reparation	reparación
repetition	repetición

reproduction . . . . reproducción

reputation . . . . **reputación**

"He has a good reputation." . . . **"Él tiene una buena reputación".**

reservation . . . . reservación

resignation . . . . resignación *(meaning "yielding";*
"job resignation" is
"dimisión")

resolution . . . . resolución

respiration . . . . respiración

restitution . . . . restitución

restoration . . . . restauración

restriction . . . . restricción

resurrection . . . . resurrección

retention . . . . retención

retraction . . . . retracción

retribution . . . . retribución

revelation . . . . revelación

revolution . . . . **revolución**

rotation . . . . rotación

salvation . . . . salvación

sanction . . . . sanción

satisfaction . . . . **satisfacción**

"It gives me a lot of satisfaction." . . . **"Me da mucha satisfacción".**

saturation . . . . saturación

secretion . . . . secreción

section . . . . sección

sedation . . . . sedación

sedition . . . . sedición

seduction . . . . seducción

segmentation . . . . segmentación

segregation . . . . segregación

selection . . . . selección

self-destruction . . . . autodestrucción

sensation . . . . sensación

separation . . . . separación

simplification. . . . . simplificación
simulation. . . . . simulación
situation . . . . **situación**
solution . . . . **solución**
sophistication . . . . sofisticación
specialization . . . . especialización
specification . . . . especificación
speculation. . . . . especulación
stabilization . . . . estabilización
station . . . . **estación**
sterilization. . . . . esterilización
stimulation . . . . estimulación *(more commonly "estímulo")*

stipulation. . . . . estipulación
sublimation. . . . . sublimación
subordination . . . . subordinación
substitution . . . . sustitución
subtraction . . . . sustracción
superstition . . . . superstición
supposition . . . . suposición
synchronization. . . . . sincronización

temptation . . . . tentación
termination . . . . terminación
tradition . . . . **tradición**
    "It's a long tradition." . . . . . . **"Es una larga tradición".**
transaction . . . . transacción
transcription . . . . transcripción
transformation. . . . . transformación
transition . . . . transición
trepidation . . . . trepidación
tribulation. . . . . tribulación

unification . . . . unificación

vacation . . . . vacación
vacillation . . . . vacilación
validation . . . . validación
variation . . . . variación
vegetation . . . . vegetación
veneration . . . . veneración
ventilation . . . . ventilación
verification . . . . verificación
vibration . . . . vibración
vindication . . . . vindicación
violation . . . . violación
visualization . . . . visualización
vocalization . . . . vocalización
vocation . . . . vocación

Una las palabras que están relacionadas o que son sinónimos.

1. información	sentimiento
2. dirección	a la derecha
3. estación	fiesta
4. nación	noticias
5. emoción	país
6. solución	tren
7. celebración	resultado

Escuche y lea el cuento. Responda las siguientes preguntas, usando oraciones completas.

En la <u>estación</u> de Salamanca, Juan y Angélica ven un anuncio (a sign) **para una gran <u>celebración</u> en la plaza principal para esa noche. Leen la <u>información</u> y comprenden que esta fiesta será grande. Angélica no quiere ir porque no se siente bien** (she doesn't feel well)**. Juan dice, "Así me pagas el favor". Angélica ve que la <u>reacción</u> de Juan es fuerte y ella dice, "Está bien, vamos". Juan dice, "Pero qué <u>situación</u> perfecta para conocer esta bella ciudad y su cocina". La <u>reacción</u> de Angélica es más sobria** (subdued)**. Ella dice, "Sí, nos encontramos en una buena <u>posición</u> aquí". Al final de la fiesta Juan está más tranquilo. Él dice, "Angélica, comí y bebí demasiado, debo irme a dormir".**

1. ¿Dónde ven el anuncio para la celebración?

2. ¿Cómo será esta fiesta?

3. ¿Por qué es importante la celebración para Juan?

4. ¿Cómo es la reacción de Angélica?

5. Al final de la fiesta, ¿en qué condición se encuentra Juan?

Chapter 24

Many English words that end in "–ty" correspond to "–dad" in Spanish.

Spanish words ending in "–dad" are usually feminine nouns. For example,

the responsibility = *la responsabilidad*

ENGLISH . . . . SPANISH

All words and phrases in **bold** *are on* **Track 24** *of the accompanying audio.*

ability . . . . habilidad
abnormality . . . . anormalidad
acceptability . . . . aceptabilidad
accessibility . . . . accesibilidad
activity . . . . **actividad**
actuality . . . . actualidad *(meaning "current events")*
adaptability . . . . adaptabilidad
admissibility . . . . admisibilidad
adversity . . . . adversidad
affinity . . . . afinidad
aggressivity . . . . agresividad
agility . . . . agilidad
alacrity . . . . alacridad
ambiguity . . . . ambigüedad
amenity . . . . amenidad
amorality . . . . amoralidad
animosity . . . . animosidad
annuity . . . . anualidad
antiquity . . . . antigüedad
anxiety . . . . **ansiedad**
  "You have too much anxiety." . . . **"Tienes demasiada ansiedad".**
applicability . . . . aplicabilidad

artificiality . . . . artificialidad
atrocity. . . . . atrocidad
austerity . . . . austeridad
authenticity. . . . . autenticidad
authority. . . . . autoridad

banality . . . . banalidad
barbarity . . . . barbaridad
bisexuality . . . . bisexualidad
brevity . . . . brevedad
brutality . . . . brutalidad

calamity . . . . calamidad
capacity . . . . capacidad
cavity. . . . . cavidad *(for teeth, use "caries")*
celebrity . . . . **celebridad**
 "Paul Newman is   **"Paul Newman es una**
 a celebrity." . . . . **celebridad".**
centrality . . . . centralidad
charity . . . . caridad
chastity. . . . . castidad
Christianity . . . . Cristiandad
city . . . . ciudad
civility . . . . civilidad
clarity. . . . . claridad
collectivity. . . . . colectividad
commodity . . . . comodidad *(meaning "comfort,"*
             "convenience")
communicability . . . . comunicabilidad
community . . . . **comunidad**
compatibility . . . . compatibilidad
complexity . . . . complejidad
complicity. . . . . complicidad
conductivity . . . . conductividad
conformity . . . . conformidad
continuity . . . . continuidad

cordiality . . . . cordialidad
corruptibility . . . . corruptibilidad
creativity . . . . **creatividad**
credibility . . . . credibilidad
cruelty . . . . crueldad
culpability. . . . . culpabilidad
curiosity . . . . **curiosidad**

debility. . . . . debilidad
deformity . . . . deformidad
density . . . . densidad
difficulty . . . . **dificultad**
dignity . . . . dignidad
discontinuity . . . . discontinuidad
dishonesty . . . . deshonestidad
disparity. . . . . disparidad
diversity . . . . diversidad
divinity. . . . . divinidad
divisibility. . . . . divisibilidad
domesticity . . . . domesticidad
duality . . . . dualidad
duplicity . . . . duplicidad
durability . . . . durabilidad

elasticity. . . . . elasticidad
electricity . . . . **electricidad**
    "There is no electricity." . . . . . **"No hay electricidad".**
eligibility . . . . elegibilidad
enormity. . . . . enormidad
entity . . . . entidad
equality . . . . igualdad
equanimity . . . . ecuanimidad
equity. . . . . equidad
eternity. . . . . eternidad
eventuality . . . . eventualidad
exclusivity. . . . . exclusividad

expressivity . . . . expresividad

extremity . . . . extremidad

facility . . . . facilidad *(meaning "talent" or "ease")*

faculty . . . . *facultad *(only used for "university
                                                    department," "right,"
                                                    or "ability")*

fallibility . . . . falibilidad

falsity . . . . falsedad

familiarity . . . . familiaridad

fatality . . . . fatalidad *(also used for "misfortune,"
                                                    "disaster")*

felicity . . . . felicidad

femininity . . . . feminidad

ferocity . . . . ferocidad

fertility . . . . fertilidad

festivity . . . . festividad

fidelity . . . . fidelidad

finality . . . . finalidad *(meaning "goal,"
                                                    "objective")*

flexibility . . . . **flexibilidad**

   "It's important   **"Es importante**

    to have flexibility." . . . . **tener flexibilidad".**

formality . . . . formalidad

fragility . . . . fragilidad

fraternity . . . . fraternidad

frugality . . . . frugalidad

functionality . . . . funcionalidad

futility . . . . futilidad

generality . . . . generalidad

generosity . . . . **generosidad**

governability . . . . gobernabilidad

gratuity . . . . gratuidad *(meaning "free,"
                                                    "no charge")*

gravity . . . . gravedad

heterosexuality	heterosexualidad
hilarity	hilaridad
homosexuality	homosexualidad
honesty	honestidad
hospitality	hospitalidad
hostility	hostilidad
humanity	humanidad
humidity	humedad
humility	humildad
hyperactivity	hiperactividad
identity	**identidad**
illegality	ilegalidad
illegibility	ilegibilidad
immensity	inmensidad
immortality	inmortalidad
immunity	inmunidad
impartiality	imparcialidad
impassivity	impasibilidad
impermeability	impermeabilidad
impiety	impiedad
impossibility	**imposibilidad**
improbability	improbabilidad
impropriety	impropiedad
inactivity	inactividad
incapacity	incapacidad
incompatibility	incompatibilidad
inconformity	inconformidad
incredulity	incredulidad
indignity	indignidad
individuality	individualidad
inequality	desigualdad
inevitability	inevitabilidad
infallibility	infalibilidad
inferiority	inferioridad
infertility	infertilidad

infidelity . . . . infidelidad
infinity . . . . infinidad
infirmity . . . . enfermedad
inflexibility . . . . inflexibilidad
informality . . . . informalidad
ingenuity . . . . ingenuidad *(meaning "innocence,"*
"naiveté")

iniquity. . . . . iniquidad
insecurity . . . . inseguridad
insensitivity . . . . insensibilidad
insincerity. . . . . insinceridad
instability . . . . inestabilidad
integrity . . . . integridad
intensity . . . . **intensidad**
intolerability . . . . intolerabilidad
invariability. . . . . invariabilidad
invisibility . . . . invisibilidad
invulnerability . . . . invulnerabilidad
irrationality. . . . . irracionalidad
irregularity . . . . irregularidad
irresponsibility. . . . . irresponsabilidad

legality. . . . . legalidad
legibility . . . . legibilidad
liberty . . . . **libertad
"Here's the Statue   **"La Estatua de la Libertad**
of Liberty." . . . . **está aquí".**
locality. . . . . localidad
longevity . . . . longevidad
loyalty . . . . *lealtad

magnanimity. . . . . magnanimidad
majesty . . . . *majestad
malleability. . . . . maleabilidad
marginality . . . . marginalidad
masculinity . . . . masculinidad

maternity . . . . maternidad
mediocrity . . . . mediocridad
mentality . . . . mentalidad
mobility . . . . movilidad
modality. . . . . modalidad
modernity. . . . . modernidad
monstrosity . . . . monstruosidad
morality . . . . moralidad
mortality. . . . . mortalidad
multiplicity . . . . multiplicidad
mutability . . . . mutabilidad
mutuality. . . . . mutualidad
municipality . . . . municipalidad

Nativity . . . . Navidad *(meaning "Christmas")*
necessity. . . . . **necesidad**
negativity . . . . negatividad
neutrality . . . . neutralidad
normality . . . . normalidad
notoriety. . . . . notoriedad
novelty . . . . novedad

obesity . . . . obesidad
objectivity. . . . . objetividad
obscenity . . . . obscenidad
obscurity . . . . oscuridad *(meaning "darkness")*
opportunity. . . . . **oportunidad**
originality. . . . . originalidad

parity. . . . . paridad
partiality. . . . . parcialidad
particularity . . . . particularidad
passivity. . . . . pasividad
paternity. . . . . paternidad
peculiarity . . . . peculiaridad

penalty. . . . . penalidad *(meaning "suffering,"*
"hardship")

permeability . . . . permeabilidad

permissibility. . . . . permisibilidad

perpetuity. . . . . perpetuidad

perplexity . . . . perplejidad

personality . . . . **personalidad**

perversity . . . . perversidad

piety . . . . piedad *(meaning "pity")*

plasticity. . . . . plasticidad

plurality . . . . pluralidad

polarity . . . . polaridad

popularity. . . . . popularidad

possibility . . . . **posibilidad**

    "There's a lot of possibility." . . . **"Hay mucha posibilidad"**.

posterity . . . . posteridad

priority . . . . prioridad

probability . . . . probabilidad

productivity. . . . . productividad

profundity. . . . . profundidad

promiscuity. . . . . promiscuidad

property. . . . . propiedad

prosperity. . . . . prosperidad

proximity . . . . proximidad

puberty . . . . pubertad

publicity. . . . . publicidad *(also used for "advertising")*

punctuality . . . . puntualidad

quality . . . . **calidad**

quantity . . . . **cantidad**

rationality. . . . . racionalidad

reality . . . . realidad

regularity . . . . regularidad

relativity . . . . relatividad

respectability . . . . respetabilidad

responsibility. . . . . **responsabilidad**

"Whose responsibility is it?" . . . **"¿De quién es la responsabilidad?"**

sanity. . . . . sanidad *(meaning "general health")*
security. . . . . seguridad
selectivity . . . . selectividad
senility . . . . senilidad
sensibility . . . . sensibilidad
sensitivity . . . . sensibilidad
sensuality . . . . sensualidad
serenity . . . . serenidad
severity. . . . . severidad
sexuality. . . . . sexualidad
similarity. . . . . similaridad
simplicity . . . . simplicidad
sincerity . . . . sinceridad
singularity. . . . . singularidad
sobriety . . . . sobriedad
society . . . . sociedad
solidarity . . . . solidaridad
solubility. . . . . solubilidad
speciality . . . . **especialidad**
spirituality. . . . . espiritualidad
spontaneity. . . . . espontaneidad
stability . . . . estabilidad
sterility . . . . esterilidad
subjectivity . . . . subjetividad
superficiality . . . . superficialidad
superiority . . . . superioridad

temerity . . . . temeridad
temporality . . . . temporalidad
tenacity . . . . tenacidad
tonality. . . . . tonalidad
totality . . . . totalidad

tranquility . . . . tranquilidad
trinity . . . . trinidad
triviality . . . . trivialidad

ubiquity . . . . ubicuidad
uniformity . . . . uniformidad
unity . . . . unidad
universality . . . . universalidad
university . . . . **universidad**
   "It's a good university." . . . . . **"Es una buena universidad".**
utility . . . . utilidad *(meaning "usefulness")*

vanity. . . . . vanidad
variability . . . . variabilidad
variety . . . . variedad
velocity . . . . velocidad
verity . . . . verdad *(meaning "truth")*
versatility . . . . versatilidad
viability . . . . viabilidad
vicinity . . . . vecindad
virginity . . . . virginidad
virility. . . . . virilidad
virtuality . . . . virtualidad
viscosity . . . . viscosidad
visibility . . . . **visibilidad**
vitality . . . . vitalidad
vivacity. . . . . vivacidad
volatility . . . . volatilidad
voracity . . . . voracidad
vulgarity. . . . . vulgaridad
vulnerability . . . . vulnerabilidad

these words end in –tad, not –dad

Una las palabras que están relacionadas o que son sinónimos.

1. calidad	excelencia
2. creatividad	luz
3. personalidad	abundancia
4. universidad	arte
5. cantidad	carácter
6. electricidad	infinito
7. eternidad	profesora

Escuche y lea el cuento. Responda las siguientes preguntas, usando oraciones completas.

La última ciudad para Juan y Angélica es La Coruña. Angélica está muy entusiasmada; dice que La Coruña es una <u>ciudad</u> con mucha <u>creatividad</u> y <u>actividad</u>. Juan dice que le gusta mucho la <u>personalidad</u> de este lugar. No tienen mucha <u>dificultad</u> en andar por las calles y puentes (bridges) **de la <u>ciudad</u>. La Coruña es una bella <u>comunidad</u> y ellos permanecen allí** (they stay there) **por cuatro días. Un día Angélica cree ver** (she thinks she sees) **una <u>celebridad</u>: Antonio Banderas. Pero Juan dice que es una <u>imposibilidad</u>, porque Banderas está filmando una película en Suiza. Antes de partir a casa, Juan dice, "Angélica, tengo una pregunta, podemos vivir aquí en La Coruña algún día?" Angélica responde, "Sí, sí, hay muchas <u>posibilidades</u> para nosotros aquí. Veremos...".**

1. ¿Qué dice Angélica de La Coruña?

2. ¿Qué le gusta a Juan de esta ciudad?

3. ¿Tienen dificultad en andar por La Coruña?

4. ¿Angélica ve a una celebridad?

5. ¿Quiere Angélica vivir en La Coruña algún día? ¿Qué dice?

1A.

1. animal: gato
2. personal: privado
3. artificial: sintético
4. crucial: importante
5. ideal: perfecto
6. legal: contrato
7. final: terminar

1B.

1. Juan y Angélica son de Bilbao.
2. Juan quiere hacer un viaje internacional.
3. Angélica quiere hacer un viaje nacional.
4. Juan dice que la idea de Angélica no es original.
5. Según Juan, el tío de Angélica es demasiado formal y tradicional.

2A.

1. fragancia: perfume
2. distancia: lejos
3. perseverancia: constancia
4. tolerancia: paciencia
5. arrogancia: soberbia
6. ambulancia: hospital
7. importancia: significado

2B.

1. Juan habla de la importancia de no gastar mucho.
2. Juan no tiene mucha tolerancia hacia el mundo "chic".
3. La perseverancia será necesaria.
4. Sí, Angélica entiende la importancia de no gastar mucho dinero.
5. Juan responde, "Veremos".

3A.

1. ignorante: desconocedor
2. elegante: fino
3. importante: esencial
4. elefante: animal
5. arrogante: pretencioso
6. flagrante: evidente
7. restaurante: cafetería

3B.

1. Van a Barcelona
2. Angélica piensa que la gente de Barcelona es arrogante.
3. Juan dice que el modo de vestir de la gente de Barcelona es muy elegante.
4. Juan dice que la historia de Barcelona es muy importante.
5. El restaurante de Andrés se llama El Elefante Rojo.

4A.

1. cardiovascular: corazón
2. regular: constante
3. singular: único
4. circular: redondo
5. similar: parecido
6. dólar: moneda
7. nuclear: atómico

4B.

1. Van a una lección de italiano mientras están en Barcelona.
2. Andrés estudia italiano porque el italiano es muy popular en Ibiza, y quiere trabajar en Ibiza.
3. El profesor habla de muchos verbos irregulares.
4. Los tres amigos hablan de la diferencia entre el singular y el plural en el italiano.
5. No, Angélica piensa que el italiano es muy irregular (difícil).

INSTANT Spanish Vocabulary Builder

5A.

1. aniversario: cumpleaños

2. salario: dinero

3. necesario: vital

4. vocabulario: palabras

5. itinerario: ruta

6. ordinario: común

7. contrario: opuesto

5B.

1. El itinerario de Juan y Angélica es muy intenso en Barcelona.

2. Angélica quiere comprar un diario.

3. Angélica escribe mucho/todo/cada detalle en su diario.

4. Juan dice que el ritmo es extraordinario.

5. Según Juan, no es necesario escribir cada detalle en el diario.

6A.

1. flexible: elástico

2. terrible: horrible

3. probable: posible

4. estable: seguro

5. inflexible: rígido

6. miserable: infeliz

7. adorable: bonito

6B.

1. Después de Barcelona van a Valencia.

2. Angélica piensa que Juan es muy irresponsable.

3. Juan dice que Angélica es inflexible.

4. Angélica piensa que es (bastante) improbable que regresen a Valencia algún día.

5. Al final, Angélica pregunta si será posible comprar los boletos en Valencia.

7A.

1. correcto: bien
2. perfecto: ideal
3. incorrecto: mal
4. dialecto: idioma
5. acto: teatro
6. aspecto: parte
7. insecto: mosca

7B.

1. Tomaron el tren directo de Barcelona a Valencia.
2. Angélica piensa que no es el lugar correcto porque no comprende nada.
3. Angélica no comprende el español en Valencia porque hay
   un acento fuerte.
4. El contacto de Juan en Valencia se llama Alfonso.
5. La salsa de Alfonso estuvo perfecta.

8A.

1. paciencia: esperar
2. conferencia: reunión
3. residencia: casa
4. diferencia: distinción
5. violencia: guerra
6. evidencia: prueba
7. independencia: liberación

8B.

1. Alfonso dice que él y su novia van al baile mañana por la noche.
2. Según Angélica la persistencia y diligencia ayudan.
3. Juan piensa que el baile será una buena experiencia.
4. A Juan el baile le causa indiferencia.
5. Juan pide disculpas por su impaciencia.

9A.

1. permanente: fijo
2. reciente: nuevo
3. diferente: distinto
4. presidente: jefe
5. evidente: obvio
6. residente: habitante
7. presente: actual

9B.

1. Angélica recibe un mensaje urgente.
2. Diego es el presidente de una compañia médica.
3. Angélica dice que su primo es diferente (inteligente/un médico competente).
4. Según Angélica, Diego es muy inteligente.
5. Al final Juan dice, "Está bien, veremos".

10A.

1. biología: vida
2. radiología: rayos X
3. tecnología: computadora
4. trilogía: tres
5. estrategia: plan
6. cronología: historia
7. geología: tierra

10B.

1. Diego tiene mucha energía.
2. Los muchachos no tienen alergia al café.
3. Diego habla de nuevas tecnologías.
4. Juan nunca ha estudiado radiología.
5. Angélica no estudia psicología.

11A.

1. pragmático: práctico
2. tráfico: carros
3. auténtico: verdadero
4. específico: detalles
5. electrónico: estéreo
6. clásico: intemporal
7. romántico: amoroso

11B.

1. Hay mucho tráfico.
2. Angélica dice que el tren es mejor porque no es muy romántico pasar las vacaciones dentro de un carro.
3. Van a algunos museos artísticos.
4. Alicante es mágico por la noche.
5. Alicante es una ciudad fantástica.

12A.

1. típico: usual
2. idéntico: igual
3. práctico: pragmático
4. biográfico: personal
5. diabólico: demoníaco
6. clínico: médico
7. crítico: importante

12B.

1. Juan quiere permanacer en Alicante.
2. Angélica quiere viajar de una manera lógica.
3. Sí, Angélica es siempre práctica.
4. Van a la Costa del Sol.
5. Angélica dice, "Tu también quieres ir a la Costa del Sol, ¿verdad?"

13A.

1. rápido: veloz
2. tímido: introvertido
3. estúpido: idiota
4. ácido: limón
5. frígido: helado
6. árido: seco
7. espléndido: maravilloso

13B.

1. Angélica dice que es un plan estúpido.
2. Juan piensa que es un plan (idea) espléndido.
3. Hace calor (muy húmedo) durante el viaje.
4. Angélica le compra un poco de antiácido para Juan cuando él se siente mal.
5. El farmacéutico dice que debe beber mucho líquido y no comer comida ácida.

14A.

1. turismo: vacaciones
2. comunismo: Karl Marx
3. patriotismo: nación
4. atletismo: olímpico
5. terrorismo: bomba
6. optimismo: positivo
7. criticismo: comentario

14B.

1. Sí, hay mucho turismo en la Costa del Sol.
2. El fascismo comenzó durante los años treinta.
3. Angélica lee sobre la influencia del comunismo y del socialismo en España.
4. Ellos hablan sobre el patriotismo español.
5. Al final Juan dice, "¡Tomemos un helado!"

15A.

1. artista: cantante
2. dentista: diente
3. turista: pasaporte
4. pesimista: negativo
5. idealista: positivo
6. finalista: campeón
7. capitalista: dinero

15B.

1. El muchacho es dentista.
2. Sí, los nuevos amigos de Juan y Angélica viajan a menudo.
3. Angélica tiene una lista de preguntas.
4. El dentista es pesimista y es realista.
5. La artista es optimista y es idealista.

16A.

1. creativo: imaginativo
2. consecutivo: siguiente
3. negativo: pesimista
4. positivo: optimista
5. competitivo: ganador
6. productivo: eficiente
7. motivo: causa

16B.

1. Juan había escuchado muchas cosas negativas sobre Andalucía.
2. Juan piensa que (ve) Andalucía es absolutamente fascinante.
3. Angélica tiene una impresión positiva de Andalucía.
4. El pueblo de Jerez es poco activo pero muy acogedor.
5. Pasan dos días consecutivos allí.

17A.

1. instrumento: guitarra

2. apartamento: renta

3. momento: instante

4. documento: papel

5. tratamiento: medicina

6. segmento: parte

7. monumento: héroes

17B.

1. El argumento en camino hacia el norte es si ir a Córdoba o no.

2. El tío de Angélica vive en Córdoba.

3. Su tío es profesor.

4. Juan no quiere ir a Córdoba porque el tío de Angélica siempre tiene algún comentario sobre el compartamiento de ellos (él es muy formal y nunca da un halago).

5. Sí, al final, deciden ir a Córdoba.

18A.

1. motor: coche

2. color: verde

3. favor: gracias

4. terror: horror

5. autor: libro

6. inventor: patente

7. exterior: afuera

18B.

1. Angélica nota el terror en la cara de Juan.

2. Juan dice, "¡Qué error venir aquí!" sobre la decisión de ir a Córdoba.

3. Juan dice, "Dime que no debo ir a esa fiesta".

4. No, el actor no es famoso.

5. No, el senador es muy, muy viejo.

19A.

1. accesorio: aretes
2. territorio: zona
3. dormitorio: cama
4. laboratorio: experimento
5. observatorio: telescopio
6. derogatorio: insulto
7. introductorio: prólogo

19B.

1. Después de Córdoba van a Sevilla.
2. Juan hubiera preferido un hostal.
3. Juan dice que la fiesta fue peor que el purgatorio.
4. No, no es verdad que su presencia no era obligatoria.
5. No, Juan no responde al último comentario contradictorio de Angélica.

20A.

1. curioso: inquisitivo
2. famoso: celebridad
3. delicioso: sabroso
4. misterioso: suspenso
5. furioso: enojado
6. precioso: diamante
7. espacioso: amplio

20B.

1. Quieren pasar un fin de semana ambicioso en Sevilla.
2. Sevilla es famosa por los churros deliciosos.
3. El amigo de Juan le dijo que hay un aire misterioso allí.
4. En la Universidad de Sevilla hay un programa famoso de lenguas extranjeras.
5. Su hotel es muy espacioso.

21A.

1. confusión: caos
2. misión: objetivo
3. televisión: antena
4. explosión: bomba
5. pasión: amor
6. precisión: exactitud
7. visión: ojo

21B.

1. La misión de Angélica es encontrar un plato de cerámica.
2. Quiere el plato para su colección.
3. Angélica dice que su decisión es final.
4. Juan tiene la impresión de que Angélica no está bromeando.
5. Había un poco de confusión con todas las callejuelas y callejones.

22A.

1. crisis: dificultad
2. tuberculosis: enfermedad
3. énfasis: acento
4. parálisis: inmovilidad
5. hipnosis: soñar
6. metamorfosis: cambio
7. análisis: estudio

22B.

1. No ponen mucho énfasis en el giro turístico porque ya conocen Madrid bastante bien.
2. Carlos escribe la tesis sobre la crisis financiera del tercer mundo.
3. Sí, Carlos habla largo y tendido sobre su análisis.
4. No, Carlos no tiene una buena hipótesis para su tesis.
5. Carlos pregunta a Juan, "¿Puedes ayudarme?"

23A.

1. información: noticias
2. dirección: a la derecha
3. estación: tren
4. nación: país
5. emoción: sentimiento
6. solución: resultado
7. celebración: fiesta

23B.

1. Ven el anuncio para la celebración en la estación de Salamanca.
2. Esta fiesta será grande.
3. La celebración es importante para Juan porque es la situación perfecta para conocer Salamanca y su cocina.
4. La reacción de Angélica es más sobria.
5. Al final de la fiesta Juan está mas tranquilo.

24A.

1. calidad: excelencia
2. creatividad: arte
3. personalidad: carácter
4. universidad: profesora
5. cantidad: abundancia
6. electricidad: luz
7. eternidad: infinito

24B.

1. Angélica dice que La Coruña es una ciudad con mucha creatividad y actividad.
2. A Juan le gusta la personalidad de esta ciudad.
3. No, no tienen dificultad en andar por La Coruña.
4. Angélica cree ver a una celebridad.
5. Angélica dice, "Sí, hay muchas posibilidades para nosostros aquí… veremos".

AUDIO TRACK LIST

Audio files available for download at:
http://www.hippocrenebooks.com/instant-spanish-vocabulary-builder.html

	English suffix	Spanish suffix
Track 1 (3:36)	–al	–al
Track 2 (2:14)	–ance	–ancia
Track 3 (2:41)	–ant	–ante
Track 4 (1:58)	–ar	–ar
Track 5 (2:36)	–ary	–ario
Track 6 (3:58)	–ble	–ble
Track 7 (2:13)	–ct	–cto
Track 8 (3:16)	–ence	–encia
Track 9 (3:01)	–ent	–ente
Track 10 (2:45)	–gy	–gía
Track 11 (4:21)	–ic	–ico
Track 12 (2:23)	–ical	–ico
Track 13 (1:46)	–id	–ido
Track 14 (3:04)	–ism	–ismo
Track 15 (3:16)	–ist	–ista
Track 16 (3:19)	–ive	–ivo
Track 17 (2:20)	–ment	–mento
Track 18 (3:18)	–or	–or
Track 19 (1:50)	–ory	–orio
Track 20 (2:48)	–ous	–oso
Track 21 (3:03)	–sion	–sión
Track 22 (2:13)	–sis	–sis
Track 23 (5:05)	–tion	–ción
Track 24 (3:57)	–ty	–dad
Track 25 (1:18)	Pronunciation Guide	

.

CPSIA information can be obtained
at www.ICGtesting.com
Printed in the USA
LVHW011406011218
598891LV00005B/8